70114539

DOES SATAN STILL APPROACH THE WOMAN AS THE WEAKER VESSEL FOR IMMORAL LIFESTYLE CHANGES?

PRAYING FOR GOD BOOKS

PAT MURRY

authorHOUSE®

AuthorHouse™
1663 Liberty Drive
Bloomington, IN 47403
www.authorhouse.com
Phone: 1 (800) 839-8640

© 2016 Pat Murry. All rights reserved.

No part of this book may be reproduced, stored in a retrieval system, or
transmitted by any means without the written permission of the author.

Published by AuthorHouse   04/19/2016

ISBN: 978-1-5049-8236-8 (sc)
ISBN: 978-1-5049-8235-1 (e)

Print information available on the last page.

Any people depicted in stock imagery provided by Thinkstock are models,
and such images are being used for illustrative purposes only.
Certain stock imagery © Thinkstock.

This book is printed on acid-free paper.

Because of the dynamic nature of the Internet, any web addresses or
links contained in this book may have changed since publication and
may no longer be valid. The views expressed in this work are solely those
of the author and do not necessarily reflect the views of the publisher,
and the publisher hereby disclaims any responsibility for them.

KJV
Scripture quotations marked KJV are from the Holy Bible, King James
Version (Authorized Version). First published in 1611. Quoted from the KJV
Classic Reference Bible, Copyright © 1983 by The Zondervan Corporation.

CONTENTS

Come now, and let us reason together, saith the LORD: though your sins be as scarlet, they shall be as white as snow; though they be red like crimson, they shall be as wool. Isaiah (1:18) (KJV)

ACKNOWLEDGEMENTS

I wish to thank my supporters for your willingness to explore the thoughts, and inquiry of God that fascinates the mind. It is an important effort to explore the mind of God, which is not spoken to us by our leaders. Sometimes our instructors keep us on milk too long; that's when the Holy Spirit will begin to draw us out individually that we may get to know Him personally for ourselves. It is time that we should get to know the heart and thoughts of God as He already knows our thoughts.

This book is written as a documentary, it is not about women alone as the title does suggest, but salvation also as our way back to the father after we have failed Him miserably; even though we may have known better. It also has quite a few scriptures for the person who may not have a complete understanding in how the scriptures must fit together. It is also for people who don't always have a bible handy while reading; and the written scriptures are sometimes very necessary for better understanding and for faster reading. Eliminating having to return to another book over and over again.

Using my own experience of when I first began to study the bible; I didn't understand why I had to go from one scripture to another scripture in order to get the correct understanding of how to know the scriptures. My question was why couldn't I just read the bible and just believe what it said, and why did I have to do all that! (Rebellion)! You know the script, my way or no way. Finally I read Isaiah 28:9, 10 (KJV) which was emphatic about: line upon line, line upon line, precept upon precept, precept upon precept; here a little and there a little. I also read Isaiah 34:16 which commands us to seek ye out of the book of the LORD and read.

I also read first Timothy 4:13 which said to take head to thyself; give attendance to reading, to exhortation, to doctrine.

Doctrine is a word which simply means "teaching". 2nd Timothy 3:16 said that: All scripture is given by inspiration of God… so it was important to me to bring this documentary to the public. 2nd Timothy 2:15 tells the Christian leaders to study to show thyself approved…

I pray that these pages will cause some of us to leave off the denominational teachings, and just search the scriptures to see for our own knowledge and understanding of what one must do to be saved according to the scriptures, and how to live the holiness life without the stigma of being self-righteous; but truly walking in the faith of God and not the tradition of religion.

Please don't close the book too quick, it gets more and more enlightening as we go. Hold on to your hat, you may even become angry but keep reading. Be not robbed by the devil, comfort will soon come to you.

Later in the book we will learn more about the so-called weaker vessel: it may astound you about the things we learn about that precious weaker vessel.

We are sure to learn some fundamentals of life together.

God bless you

PROLOGUE

Introduction to the thoughts of God:

All scriptures is taken from the Kings James version of the bible, and other periodicals; My approach to the subject of the fundamentals of life may be a bit unorthodox too some of you, because of the approach on things in the mind of God before time was; before man was created, and before the generation of the stars and of the heaven and the earth. Before time as we know it: this is where God worked out all matters and situations concerning time, salvation, and the death burial and resurrection of Himself; (Jesus Christ.) This is where God worked on man's salvation, knowing the ending from the beginning, as the scripture declare. Isaiah 46:10 (KJV)

All things were formed in His mind, and in His thoughts, and in His being before He spoke them into existence, bringing all things to life. God spoke everything into existence except the man, the man was created with His hand, formed, and brought to life with the breath of God.

And the Lord God formed man of the dust of the ground, and breathed into his nostrils the breath of life; and man became a living soul. Genesis 2:7 (KJV)

Thus begins the process of the life and the love of Jesus, His death, burial and resurrection of Jesus Christ: Him bringing hope, promise and salvation to many; even the evil and to the unthankful, according to Luke 6:35 (KJV) which saith,

"But love your enemies, and do good, and lend, hoping for nothing again; and your reward shall be great, and ye shall be the children of the Highest: for He is kind unto the unthankful and to the evil." Luke 6:35 (KJV)

This Introduction to the fundamentals of life, begins and ends with the mind of God before the foundation of the world.

Blessed be the God and Father of our Lord Jesus Christ, who has blessed us with all spiritual blessings in heavenly places in Christ…" Ephesian 1:3-5 (KJV)

The thoughts of God: My argument

Note

God had the world, and all of creation in His heart and in His plan of salvation before He laid the foundation of this world. Him knowing their needs and shortcomings before He created the world, or the man, and before the fall of Adam God understood all his frailties and faults, and his disobedience. Yet: He prepared a place in a time and season that we should be born, and receive salvation. That's the love of God in His heart for man that He had or would create; this great love is in His provision for us toward man. It was already in His heart to save man;

Who hath saved us, and called us with a holy calling, not according to our own works, but according to His own purpose and grace, which was given us in Christ Jesus before the world began. 2ⁿᵈ Timothy 1:9(KJV)

Not by his works which the man had done, but by the grace, and mercy of God that He would extend to all people through Christ Jesus. This is God's one great love with no upbraiding.

St. John 3: 16 (KJV)

"For God so loved the world that He gave His only begotten son, that whosoever believeth in Him should not perish, but have everlasting life.

Isaiah's gives us the prophecy of a lifetime

Isaiah 53 (KJV)

This prophecy tells us how Christ's death would serve to keep the entire creation of God from death, Christ's death would serve as the sacrifice (remedy) to keep the entire creation from eternal death, after the disobedience of Adam would occur and that death could come only to those who would not believe in the Messiah's, (Jesus Christ) death, burial and resurrection.

"Behold, my servant shall deal prudently, He shall be exalted and extolled, and be very high.

As many were astonished at thee; (at Him) His visage was so marred more than any man, and His form more than the sons of men." Isaiah 52:13- 15 (KJV)

So shall He sprinkle many nations; the kings shall shut their mouths at Him: for that which had not been told them shall they see; and that which they had not heard shall they consider." 1ˢᵗ Peter 1: 2 (KJV)

The mind of God

Explanation

What had not been told them was the mystery of the gospel which had been so long concealed.

"But as it is written, to whom He was not spoken of, they shall see: and they that have not heard shall understand." Romans 15:21 (KJV)

"Now to Him that is of power to stablish you according to my gospel, and the preaching of Jesus Christ, according to the revelation of the mystery, which was kept secret since the world began,"

"But now is made manifest, and by the scriptures of the prophets, according to the commandment of the everlasting God, made known to all nations for the obedience of faith: Romans 16:25,26 (KJV)

Then we heard Isaiah's prophecy

"For He shall grow up before Him as a tender plant, and as a root out of a dry ground: He hath no form nor comeliness; and when we shall see Him, there is no beauty that we should desire Him.

Yet this dry ground brought forth the tree of life, which bore us as fruit from a green tree, in His season. This process brought forth saints.

Surely He hath borne our griefs, and carried our sorrows, yet we did esteem Him stricken, smitten of God, and afflicted.

But He was wounded for our transgressions, He was bruised for our iniquity: the chastisement of our peace was upon Him; and with His strips we are healed.

All we like sheep have gone astray; we have turned everyone to his own way; and the Lord hath laid on Him the iniquity of us all." Isaiah 53

"He was taken from prison and from judgement: and who shall declare His generation? For He was cut off out of the land of the living: for the transgression of my people was He stricken.

Yet it pleased the LORD to bruise Him; He hath been put to grief: when thou shall make His soul an offering for sin, He shall see His seed, He shall prolong His days, and the pleasure of the LORD shall prosper in His hand." Isaiah 53:

My point: Isaiah 52, and 53 gives us the prophecy of the coming of Jesus, the Messiah: (bringing salvation to the unsaved world.) And His persecution, and death which He would suffer for man, by man: that He might bring us together reconciling all together in one body. *In unity*

"For He is our peace, who hath made both one, and hath broken down the middle wall of partition between us; Having abolished in His flesh the enmity, even the law of commandments contained in ordinances; for to make in Himself of twain one new man, so making peace; And that He might reconcile both unto God in one body by the cross, having slain the enmity thereby: And came and preached peace to you which were afar off, and to them that were nigh.

For through Him we both have access by one spirit unto the Father." Ephesians 2:14-18 (KJV)

"For through Him, Christ Jesus that is, we both, Jews and gentiles have access to Christ by one spirit, unto the Father through the Holy Ghost."

All of this is God's preparation for man before he is created, and before he harkens to the voice of his wife. **The weaker vessel.**

Remembering Matthew 26: 26-28(KJV)

Note

"And *as they were eating, Jesus took bread, and blessed it, and break it, and gave it to the disciples, and said, take, eat; this is My body. And He took the cup, and gave thanks, and gave it to them, saying, drink ye all of it; For this is my blood of the New Testament, which is shed for many for the remission of sins.*"

God's wisdom

This is God's remedy of salvation for man before the foundation of the world. This is God's mindset before He created the man, Adam. Amen? His blood would be shed for many, because all people will not believe, obey, and receive the word of God. This is God's wisdom in how to save many. This way; many again, would have the opportunity that Adam would have; to put forth their hand to partake of the tree of life the first time, and live forever: a second time. With His stripes we are healed, healed from sicknesses, brokenness, healed from sin and death. Isaiah 53: 5; 1st. Peter 2:24 -25. (KJV)

God used other men in other times for men to know, what His promises were for his future. He used the prophet, the priest and sacrifice; all these positions were held by God. The prophet would tell of future events. He also told the people what God required of them. These positions of the Old Testament concerning the law and priesthood, sacrifices, and all the position and activities that are recorded were a symbols, or type of Christ and His church, which were to come.

"Which saith, searched the scriptures; for in them ye think ye have eternal life: and they are they which testify of me." St John 5:39, (KJV)

Gods' effective plan.

God was already present in the plan of salvation, before the world was and before man was created; all the plans of Christ for man was in His prophetic plan. The words of the prophets were His; bringing man into question, warning man of his impending doom, calling man to repentance and back to the presence of the Father. Once again, the command is to choose life.

Isaiah saith 1:18-20 KJV))

"Come now, and let us reason together saith the LORD: though your sins be as scarlet, they shall be as white as snow; though they be red like crimson, they shall be as wool.

If you be willing and obedient, you shall eat the good of the land:

But if you refuse and rebel, ye shall be devoured with the sword: for the mouth of the Lord has spoken it." Return to me: is the Lord's plea unto man.

CHAPTER I

The Garden Experience

After the creation of man, God gave him, that is, the man, an opportunity for eternal life through his good choices. His first choice should have been to obey what God had said unto him; that was, to eat of every tree in the garden **except**, of the tree of knowledge of good and evil. His second choice was to eat of the tree of life: which was in the midst of the garden next to the tree of knowledge of good and evil. But as we know his choices did not serve to bring eternal life to him, or the world. Yet, God chose to create him inspite of His foreknowledge concerning his disobedience.

"And God said, let us make man in our image, after our likeness: and let them have dominion over the fish of the sea, and over the fowl of the air, and over the cattle, and over all the earth; and over every creeping thing that creepeth upon the earth." Genesis 1:26, 27 (KJV)

"So God created man in His own image, in the image of God created He him: male and female created He them.

And the Lord God planted a garden eastward in Eden; and there He put the man whom He had formed.

And out of the ground, made the Lord God to grow every tree that is pleasant to the sight, and good for food; the tree of life also in the midst of the garden, and the tree of knowledge of good and evil." Genesis 2:8, 9 (KJV)

*"And the Lord God took the man, and put him into the Garden of Eden to dress it and to keep it. **And the Lord God commanded the man, saying**, of every tree of the garden thou mayest **freely eat. But of the tree of the knowledge of good and evil, thou shall not eat of it: for in the day that thou eatest thereof thou shalt surely die." Genesis 2; 15-17 (KJV)***

Note

We know that every man has an adversary; entering into his house through the spirit of Satan from members of his own house. In this case it is the man's wife. **The weaker vessel.**

"And a man's foes shall be they of his own household." Matthew 10:36; Micah 7:6 (KJV)

"Now the serpent was more subtle than any beast of the field which the Lord God had made. And he said unto the woman, yea, hath God said, you shall not eat of every tree of the garden?

*"**Here Satan is contending with the woman as the weaker vessel: not the man, about what God said, or***

didn't say to change the law of God". Satan is gathering information, to prove and challenge her.

And the woman said unto the serpent, we may eat of the fruit of the tree of the garden:

But of the fruit of the tree which is in the midst of the garden, God hath said, ye shall not eat of it, neither shall ye touch it, least you die.

Here Satan learns that the woman didn't really understand what God actually said.

And the serpent said unto the woman, ye shall not surely die: For God doth know that in the day ye eat thereof, then your eyes shall be opened, and you shall be as gods, knowing good and evil.

And when the woman saw that the tree was good for food, and that it was pleasant to the eyes, and a tree to be desired to make one wise, she took of the fruit thereof, and did eat, and gave also unto her husband with her; and he did eat.

And the eyes of them both were opened, and they knew that they were naked: and they sewed fig leaves together, and made themselves aprons." Genesis 3:1 – 7(KJV)

Satan's accusation of God to Eve

This is a subtle, deceptive, and great evil of Satan through the woman, bringing destruction to her own house and the creation of God through disobedience. Her invitation to her husband to eat, and mainly her husband for not refusing the evil, brought death upon the entire creation of God. Adam not being deceived, agreed with the woman in her disobedience to God in the partaking of the forbidden fruit.

Please get an understanding of this, this is not a slight toward men.

The scriptures said: **by one man, it did not say by one man and one woman, but by one man, death came upon all men.**

*"**Wherefore, as by one man sin entered into the world**, and death by sin; and so death passed upon all men, for that all have sinned." Romans 5:12 (KJV)*

Adam, however, had not the reverence, fear, love nor respect for his God that Job had for his God. Adam did not fear when it came to disobeying God, as the scripture said, **Adam was not deceived**.

Note continue

Adam did not honor his God and respect Him as his Father nor his God, but Job was just the opposite. When his wife came to tempt him with a word to curse his God and die. Unlike Adam, Job refused the invitation to commit evil in the sight of the LORD; he reverence his God, loved, respected feared and honored his God, and swiftly rebuked his wife, and called her foolish. This should have been the response from Adam to his wife, as an examples to others that would follow and from Abraham this should have been the same response to his wife Sara. **The woman as the weaker vessel.**

"So went Satan forth from the presence of the LORD, and smote Job with sore boils from the sole of his foot unto his crown. And he took him a potsherd to scrape himself withal; and he sat down among the ashes.

Then his wife said unto him, dost thou still retain thine integrity? "CURSE GOD, AND DIE." But he said unto her, thou speaketh as one of the foolish women speaketh. What? Shall we receive good at the hand of God, and shall we not receive evil? In all this did not Job sin with his lips?" Job 2:7-10 (KJV)

In spite of the loss of all of Job's wealth, the death of all of his children, and the unfaithfulness of his wife, Job, being the man of integrity that every man should be, and pattern his life after, Job stayed in his faithfulness to the LORD in the time of his temptation, and his wife's interference. Adam did not remain in obedience to his God, as did Job when his wife approached him with his temptation, he was very willing to succumb to the desires of his flesh. **In all this God still offered to him salvation, a way of escape.**

If a man, or when a man wants to know what his integrity should be, and what the moral and spiritual character of a man should really look like toward God and man: let him look to Job, Joseph and Stephen, just to name a few. The scriptures said that:

Adam was first formed, then Eve.

"And Adam was not deceived, but the woman being deceived was in the transgression." 1ˢᵗ Timothy 2:13, 14 (KJV

Meaning: she broke God's Law. Yet, God called Adam to repentance though he was not deceived, this is the second step to salvation, the first step to his salvation was when Adam heard God call him while in the garden, this was the first step towards his salvation which is to hear, and to respond positively to the call of God.

Adam offered no repentance to God for his sin; this is the third step to salvation.

We see the plan of salvation being offered to Adam and Eve by God Himself: even in the Garden of Eden, and also Gods' promise and strategy of redemption in the defeat of Satan when He said:

"And I will put enmity between thee and the woman, and between thy seed and her seed; it shall bruise thy head, and thou shall bruise his heel." Genesis 3:15 (KJV)

The scriptures tells us that God called Adam, and like so many of us today, Adam didn't respond to His call. It's amazing that we can actually hear from or hear the voice of God: and won't respond to His calling. Not knowing that He is calling us to life and not unto death.

Hearing His voice

"And they heard the voice of the Lord God walking in the garden in the cool of the day: and Adam and his wife hid themselves from the presence of the Lord God amongst the trees of the garden. And the Lord God called unto Adam, and said unto him, where are thou? And he said, I heard thy voice in the garden, and I was afraid, because I was naked; and I hid myself. And He said, who told thee that thou wast naked? Hast thou eaten of the tree, whereof I commanded thee that thou shouldest not eat? And the man said, the woman whom thou gavest to be with me, she gave me of the tree, and I did eat."

And the Lord God said unto the woman, what is this that thou has done? And the woman said, the serpent beguiled me, and I did eat. Genesis 3:8-13 (KJV)

But He asked Satan not a word, because he was a deceiver, and a liar from the beginning.

"And unto Adam He said, because thou hast hearkened unto the voice of thy wife, and hast eaten of the tree…" Genesis 3:17(KJV)

It was important to God for Adam to confess his sins right then and there leading the woman or his household to repentance, also, his wife Eve, but they accused another, and confessed not their sins unto God.

Precaution

Women should not be content with a man's teaching alone, but she must solicit the ministering of the Holy Ghost in the word which she reads and hears. Just maybe we didn't get the full story from the man like Eve.

Satan, and God's remedy for man

"Ye are of your father the devil, and the lust of your father ye will do. He was a murderer from the beginning, and abode not in the truth, because there is no truth in him. When he speak he speaketh a lie, he speaketh of his own: for he is a liar, and the father of it. According to:" St. John 8:44 (KJV)

"He that committee sin is of the devil; for the devil sinneth from the beginning. For this purpose, the son of God was manifested, that he might destroy the works of the devil." 1st John 3:8, (KJV)

This same repentance and salvation process is offered unto sinners; even today. God gave a prophetic promise of life to Adam, and the world, and His eternal promise of death to Satan.

"And I will put enmity between thee and the woman, and between thy seed and her seed: it shall bruise thy head and thou shalt bruise his heel." Genesis 3:15. (KJV)

We must have law

The law was given because of transgression, it was given for the purpose of condemning the whole world of sin that all might become guilty of sin before God, including Jews.

"For until the law sin was in the world: but sin is not imputed when there is no law.

Wherefore, as by one man sin entered into the world, and death by sin; and so death passed upon all men, for that all have sinned:

AGAIN (For until the law sin was in the world: but sin is not imputed when there is no law).

Nevertheless death reigned from Adam to Moses, even over them that had not sinned after the similitude of Adam's transgression, who is the figure of Him that was to come." Roman 5:12-14 (KJV)

"Because the law worketh wrath: for where there is no law, there is no transgression." Romans 4:15(KJV)

"Wherefore, then serves the law? It was added because of transgressions, till the seed should come to whom the promise

was made; and it was ordained by angels in the hand of a mediator." Galatians 3:19. (KJV)

The law blessed us

If the law had not been given, there would not have been a way for man to be redeemed from the curse of sin, he would have had to die without a remedy for his sins, being lost forever because of sin. God could not judge Sin without a legal reason, so He added the law that all would have understanding, and knowledge of what their sins were: and what His judgments would be, and what to refrain from that we die not.

The Law told us what we were doing wrong, and convinced us that we had sin. Thank you Lord. The law also told the world what doors Adam had open when he disobeyed God's law or commandment in the garden, and what life and death would follow: a life without Christ was our reward: exposing us to eternal damnation, but the law condemning us as sinners gave us the way of escaping death and a way back to the Father. Hallelujah! *Romans 7:7-9 (KJV)*

Searching for a man to redeem man

The Scripture saith, **"*for whom He did foreknow, He also did predestinate to be conformed to the image of His son,* that He might be the firstborn among many brethren."** Romans 8:29 (KJV)

And this is how it worked:

"In the beginning was the word, the word was with God, and the Word was God.

The same was in the beginning with God. All things were made by Him; and without Him was not anything made that was made.

*"**And the Word was made flesh,** and dwelt among us, (and we beheld His glory, the glory as of the only begotten of the Father,) full of grace and truth." St. John, 1:1- 3, 10, 14*

*"Behold, a virgin shall be with child, and shall bring forth a son, and they shall call His name Emmanuel, which being interpreted, **God with us.**" St. Matthew 1:23. (KJV)*

"And being found in fashion as a man, He humbled Himself, and became obedient unto death, even the death of the cross." Philippians 2:8 (KJV)

Through this process of the unifying of the flesh with the spirit of God, it was called the son of God. Since this was God manifested in the flesh, everything that God was in the invisible Fathership was transferred into the Sonship.

For it pleased the Father that in Him should all fullness dwell; Colossian 1:19 (KJV)

For in Him dwelleth all the fullness of the Godhead bodily. Colossians. 2:9. (KJV)

God proves Himself

Now God couldn't take it upon Himself to automatically administer the work of salvation to the souls of men because He was God: This would be wilfully usurping the will of man to be saved, denying him the freewill of choice which He had given him from the beginning, and imposing on the man to do what He wanted. So God had to prove to the human race that His way was the only way that man could be saved, and would be saved. So He made a search, for our knowledge through His word to see if there was a man to stand in the gap, or as a redeemer for man and the land. He did His own personal search for our sake.

"He said, run ye to and fro through the streets of Jerusalem, and see now, and know, and seek in the broad places thereof, if you can find a man, if there be any that executed judgment, that seeketh the truth; and I will pardon it." Jeremiah 5:1 (KJV)

"And I sought for a man among them that should make up the hedge, and stand in the gap before me for the land, that I should not destroy it: but I found none." Ezekiel 22:30 (KJV)

"And He saw that there was no, man, and wondered that there was no intercessor: therefore His arm brought salvation unto Him; and His righteousness, it sustained Him." Isaiah 59:16. (KJV)

Pleading for Sodom

Abraham's plea, beginning with fifty people

"And he said unto Him, oh let not the Lord be angry, and I will speak: peradventure there shall thirty be found there, and He said, I will not do it, if I find thirty there. And he said, behold now, I have taken upon me to speak unto the Lord: peradventure there shall be twenty found there. And He said, I will not destroy it for twenty's sake. And he said, oh let not the Lord be angry, and I will speak yet but this once: peradventure ten shall be found there. And He said, I will not destroy it for ten's sake." Genesis 18:30-32(KJV)

But as we know there was not ten saints, or righteous people to be found in the city, to stand for Sodom.

The Scripture plainly tells us that God Himself made a search for a man to stand in the gap for his brother (which is mankind). However, the Scripture said there was none. When He looked for a man to stand in place for Sodom, there was not enough righteous people to be found to save man from his disastrous fate.

Questions from the Author:

After reading this book, how do you see God as creator, knowing all of your failures, and loving you inspite of all that He knows concerning you.

Reflection:

_____

_____

_____

_____

_____

_____

_____

_____

_____

_____

_____

_____

_____

_____

_____

_____

_____

_____

_____

_____

_____

CHAPTER II

All Scripture points to Christ and His redemptive process.

God Said

"And I looked, and there was none to help; and I wondered that there was none to uphold: therefore mine own arm brought salvation unto me; and my fury, it upheld me." Isaiah 63:5 (KJV)

"Whatsoever things, were written aforetime was written for our learning, that we through patience and comfort of the Scriptures might have hope." Romans 15:4(KJV)

So it was Jesus even in those Old Testament times which the scriptures spoke of; the mystery unfolds.

This is how Jesus will counter effect the deadly actions of Adam.

For without the shedding of blood there is no remission of sin, and God is a spirit and not flesh and bone." Hebrew 9:22 (KJV)

So the blood of the sacrifices under the law was not sufficient to redeem man from the works of the law.

"Jesus had been found in fashion as a man, humbled Himself and became obedient unto death, even the death of the cross." Philippians 2:8 (KJV)

"Therefore do my Father love me because I lay down my life, that I might take it again. No man taketh it from me, but I lay it down of myself. I have power to lay it down, and I have power to take it again." St. John 10:17, 18 (KJV)

"And we are witnesses of all things which He did, both in the land of the Jews, and in Jerusalem; whom they slew and hang on the tree: Him, God raised up the third day, and showed Him openly;

Not to all the people, but unto witnesses chosen before of God, even to us, who did eat and drink with Him after He rose from the dead." John 10:17, 18; Acts 10:39 – 41 (KJV)

"Jesus answered them and said unto them, destroy this temple, and in three days I will raise it up. But He spake of the temple of His body." St. John 2:19, 21(KJV)

How to find salvation.

After all that had happened in the Garden of Eden, Adam and Eve saw fit not to repent, neither confess their sins to God while they were in His presence. Having their covering removed, being found naked with the glory of God separated from them; how can we today ask God to forgive us and take us back into the fulness of His glory? For we all were in the loins of Adam partaking of his guilt.

This is of course a rhetorical question, and one of desperation and sorrow, seeing and knowing the shame of our nakedness in our sinful state. Then we remembered the message to which, saith He, REPENT! Even if we think the best times of our lives have passed us by, we've seen the error of our ways, the best things of all these years is to hear Him say:

"Come all ye that labor and are heavy laden, and I will give you rest." Matthew 11:28(KJV)

"Ho, every one that thristeth, come ye to the waters, and he that hath no money; come ye, buy, and eat; yea, come, buy wine and milk without money and without price." Isaiah 55:1 (KJV)

Again! We have an opportunity: The second time at eternal life: by partaking of the tree of life, and not the tree of the knowledge of good and evil, choosing Jesus: this time, the first time.

Now the question would be what must we do to be saved?

Step one would be to believe on the Lord Jesus Christ as Lord and saviour the one that saves. Baptism is the formula God gave to us to wash or remit our sins, by speaking the name of Jesus Christ over the candidate by faith, this application applies the blood of Jesus to our sins while the candidate is in the water.

After the water baptism; we are expected to be spotless: and being filled with the Holy Ghost no traces or stain of sin is left behind; because the history of our sins have been totally eradicated, or wiped out from before the face of God by the shed blood of His son Jesus, whereby making peace with God.

This washing is not as much to do about the water, as it is the washing in the blood, **though it is very necessary**, the water baptism symbolizing the burial (grave) but the blood in the water applies the cleansing substance or agent for the total removal **of all sins that are passed**. Romans 3:25 (KJV)

Pay special attention to these words

"Now we know that what things soever the law saith, it saith to them who are under the law: that every mouth may be stopped, and all the world may become guilty before God. Therefore by the deeds of the law there shall no flesh be justified in His sight; for by the law is the knowledge of sin. But now the righteousness of God without the law is manifested, being witnessed by the law and the prophets;

*Even the righteousness of God which is by faith of Jesus Christ unto all and upon all them that believe: for there is no difference: For all have sinned, and come short of the glory of God; Being justified freely by His grace through the redemption that is in Christ Jesus: Whom God hath set forth to be a propitiation through faith in His blood, to declare His righteousness **for the remission of sins that are past;** To* *declare, I say, at this time His righteousness: that He might be just, and the justifier of Him which believeth in Jesus."* Romans 3:19-26 *(KJV)*

So God has made a way of escape for the sinner man through the steps of salvation, and the blood of Jesus Christ; this is the process which has been appointed to us.

You might ask the question:

What does this plan of salvation have to do with the **actions of the weaker vessel?** Well, this is where her rebellion has brought us, now we must find our way back to the Father through the steps of salvation

Philip preached to the Eunuch of the one God that could save him, the Lord Jesus Christ though he didn't believe on Jesus until he heard the word spoken to him as we do, then he received salvation as we all must do. We must hear the word, believe the word which we heard, repent of our sins, be baptized in the name of the Lord Jesus Christ, for the remission of sins. (Acts 2:38) Receive the gift of the Holy Ghost and walk in the newness of life, not returning to the old lifestyle of sin and death.

Hear these word: the Eunuch had gone up to Jerusalem for to worship; but didn't find what his soul sought-after, so Philip was able to instruct him through the word of God, by the unctioning of the Holy Ghost. Acts 8:29-39 (KJV)

We all are called to repentance through the gospel of preaching, how can we hear without a preacher? Hearing the gospel convicts us of our sin, it causes us to see clearly our natural self in the worst light.

"For whosoever shall call upon the name of the Lord shall be saved. How then shall they call Him in whom they have not believed? And how shall they believe in Him of whom they have not heard? And how shall they hear without a preacher? And how shall they preach, except they be sent… So then faith cometh by hearing, and hearing the word of God." Romans 10: 13-17 (KJV)

After we hear the gospel, it is imperative to believe the gospel which we have heard of Jesus Christ, that is, of His death burial and resurrection: and all of His offering of Himself to God, in our behalf.

The Centurion

Cornelius the gentile had to hear and believe the same message that the Eunuch had to hear and believe, the message of the death, burial and resurrection of Jesus Christ. Here we have a good man that **did everything right**, **he loved the Lord mightily**, **he prayed daily he also gave alms**; but all of this is not soul saving salvation. **These are only good works**. Cornelius was not saved yet, because he had not received Christ; according to Acts 11:14-15 (KJV) But Cornelius sought salvation for himself and his house through preaching; by sending for Peter to tell him what he must do to be saved. Acts chapter 10.

"And now send men to Joppa, and call for one Simon, whose surname is Peter:

He lodgeth with one Simon a tanner, whose house is by the sea side: he shall tell thee what thou oughtest to do." Acts 10: 5, 6 (KJV)

Believing the word of God

"But when they believed Phillip preaching the things concerning the kingdom of God, and the name of Jesus Christ, they were baptized, both men and women." (Acts 8:12, 27-38 (KJV)

Hearing the word of God

"In whom you also trusted, after that you heard the word of truth, the gospel of your salvation: in whom after that you believe, you were sealed with that holy spirit of promise." Ephesians 1:13 (KJV)

Repentance from sin:

"And she shall bring forth a son, and thou shall call His name Jesus: for He shall save His people from their sins." St. Matthew 1:21(KJV)

"And saying the time is fulfilled, and the kingdom of God is at hand: repent ye, and be believed the gospel." St. Mark 1:15(KJV)

"And the times of this ignorance. God winked at; but now command all men everywhere to repent:" Acts 17: 30(KJV)

"Repent ye therefore, and be converted, that your sins may be blotted out, when the times of refreshing shall come from the presence of the Lord;" Acts 3: 19. (KJV)

Baptism in the name of Jesus.

The baptism is not just to go into the water, but is for the cleansing away of sin, by the applying of the blood through His name; that one's sins would be washed away with the promise of the Holy Ghost being given, when one completes this process.

"And Jesus came and spake unto them, saying, all power is given unto me in heaven and in earth." Matthew 28:18 (KJV)

Go ye therefore, (as a missionary)**, and teach all nations, baptizing them in the name of the Father,** which is Jesus, **and the son,** which is Jesus**, and of the Holy Ghost:** which is Jesus**, but these titles are not His name.**

We must be washed in His blood thru His name, and His name is Jesus; the one with the power to save and the name which is the power that washes away sin. St. Matthew 28:18,19 (KJV) Evangelism, baptism, receiving the Holy Ghost, speaking with new tongues, casting out devils, taken up serpents; drinking any deadly thing, are our promises which we are to receive from the Holy Ghost, after we receive Him.

"He said unto them, go ye into all the world, and preach the gospel to every creature.

He that believeth and is baptized shall be saved; but he that believeth not shall be damned.

And these signs shall follow them that believe; in my name (speak the name: Jesus) shall they cast out devils; they shall speak with new tongues;

They shall take up serpents; and if they drink any deadly thing, it shall not hurt them; they shall lay hands on the sick, and they shall recover." St. Mark 16: 15-18. (KJV)

"Then said Peter unto them, repent, and be baptized every one of you in the name of Jesus Christ for the remission of sins, and you shall receive the gift of the Holy Ghost." Acts 2:38 (KJV)

Repentance of sin

Paul demonstrates the laying on of the hands. *"And it came to pass, that, while Apollo was at Corinth, Paul, having passed through the upper coasts came to Ephesus: and finding certain disciples, he said unto them, have you received the Holy Ghost* **since ye believed?** *And they said unto him, we have not so much as heard whether there be any Holy Ghost. And he said unto them, unto what then were you baptized?*

Baptism in the name of Jesus

*And they said, unto John's baptism. Then said Paul, John verily baptized with the baptism of repentance, saying unto the people, that they **should believe on Him which should come after him, that is, on Christ Jesus.** When they heard this, they were baptized in the name of the Lord Jesus. And when Paul had laid his hands upon them, the Holy Ghost came on them; and they spake with tongues, and prophesied. And all the men were about twelve." Acts 19:1-6 (KJV)*

Baptism of the Holy Ghost.

The baptism of the Holy Spirit is never administered to just anybody, but only to those that believe and have accepted Jesus as both Lord and Christ: It is afterwards, after **any man's** repentance, and acceptance of the Messiah: not only to the gentiles but also to the lost sheep of the household of Israel. As was spoken by the Old Testament prophets.

"And I will pour upon the house of David, and upon the inhabitants of Jerusalem, the spirit of grace and of supplication: and they shall look upon me whom they have pierced, and they shall mourn for Him, as one mourn for his only son, and shall be in bitterness for Him, as one that is in bitterness for his firstborn. In that day there shall be a fountain opened to the house of David, and to the inhabitants of Jerusalem for sin, and for uncleanness." Zachariah 12:10, 13:1 (KJV)

Then Peter said unto them, repent, and be baptized every one of you in the name of Jesus Christ for the remission of sins, and you shall receive the gift of the Holy Ghost. Acts 2:38(KJV)

And it shall come to pass afterward, that I will pour out my Spirit upon all flesh; and your sons and your daughters shall prophesy: your old men shall dream dreams, your young men shall see visions:

And also upon the servants and upon the handmaiden in those days will I pour out my Spirit. Pour means to baptize, (symbolizing Spirit or water). Joel 2:28, 29 (KJV)

"And it shall come to pass, that whosoever shall call on the name of the Lord shall be delivered: for in Mount Zion and in Jerusalem shall be deliverance, as the Lord has said, and in the remnant whom the Lord shall call. At the 2nd coming of Christ, Israel will be gathered to Palestine. And He shall send His angels with a great sound of a trumpet, and they shall gather together His elect from the four winds, from one end of heaven to the other." Joel 2:32 Matthew 24:31 (KJV)

Coming forth

We have looked at Jesus in His invisible form in Genesis, and in the Law of Moses. We've heard about Him from the Psalms, and the prophets. We've talked about salvation and the Holy Ghost, the gospels, God in creation, the fall of man, and God's plan for man's future. We saw Him in Genesis 1: 1 as creator, Elohim, we saw Him as the word, in St. John 1: 1 now we would see Him as a babe, through St. Matthew's eyes. St. Matthew presents Him to us as the king of the Jews, the one that would sit upon the throne of His father David.

Now we speak of Jesus on this wise:

"St. Matthew 1:1 the book of the generation of Jesus Christ, the son of David, the son of Abraham. Abraham begat Isaac: and Isaac begat Jacob: Jacob begat Judas and his brethren. And Jacob begat Joseph the husband of Mary of whom was born Jesus: who is called Christ." Matthew 1:1, 2, 16. (KJV)

Isaiah's prophecies said: *"unto us a child is born, unto us a son is given: and the government shall be upon His shoulder: **and His name shall be called** wonderful, counselor, **the mighty God**, the everlasting **Father,** the Prince of peace."*

"Isaiah calls this child that is born, the mighty God, *God over all,* **he also calls this son that is given***: the* **everlasting Father***, creator, Elohim." Isaiah 9:6; 7:14(KJV)*

Jesus Christ. The name Jesus is from the Greek and Latin for the Hebrew" Jeshua" (Jeshua), which means **the Lord is salvation**. Christ is from the Greek for the Hebrew Messiah, meaning the anointed one.

"Now the birth of Jesus Christ was on this wise: when as His mother Mary was espoused to Joseph, before they came together, she was found with child of the Holy Ghost.

Then Joseph her husband, being a just man, and not willing to make her a public example, was reminded to put her away privately." Matthew 1:18-19(KJV)

Coming forth

*"But while he thought on these things, behold, the angel of the LORD appeared unto him in a dream, saying, Joseph, thou son of David, fear not to take unto thee Mary thy wife: for that which is conceived in her is of the Holy Ghost. And she shall bring forth a son, and thou shall called His name Jesus: for He shall save His people from their sins. Now all this was done, that it might be fulfilled which was spoken of the LORD by the prophet, saying, Behold, a virgin shall be with child, and shall bring forth a son, and they shall call His name **Emmanuel, which being interpreted is, God with us.**" Matthew 1:1 – 23 (KJV)*

This is the path to salvation.

"Testifying both to the Jews, and also to the Greeks, repentance toward God, and faith toward our Lord Jesus Christ". Acts 20:21. (KJV)

It is most important to repent to God, because it is a requirement of God. First we heard the gospel, then we believe what we heard, after that, we apologize by asking for forgiveness with a sincere repentant heart. This is the beginning of our salvation. When we realize and admit that we have a need of forgiveness, and repentance, and believe on Jesus Christ as our Savior; the one who can save the whole world, it is necessary that every man must confess Christ, as it was necessary for Peter in the beginning.

"When Jesus came into the coast of Caesarea Philippi, He asked His disciples, saying, whom do men say that I the son of man am?

And they said, some say that thou our John the Baptist: some, Elias; and others, Jeremias, or one of the prophets. But He said unto them, but **whom say ye that I am?**

Jesus was asking them to acknowledge before Him, who He was, if they knew.

This is a necessary requirement: individually, and personally that each individual know for themselves who Jesus is, as it is also today in our confession, we must know the Savior, **and His name.**

And Simon Peter answered and said, thou art the Christ, the son of the living God.

And Jesus answered and said unto him, Blessed art thou, Simon bar Jonah for flesh and blood hath not revealed it unto thee, but my Father which is in heaven.

And I say also unto thee, that thou art Peter, and upon this rock (upon this revelation of who I am) I will build my church; and the gates of hell shall not prevail against it.

And I will give unto thee, the keys of the kingdom of heaven: and whatsoever thou shall bind on earth shall be bound in heaven: and whatsoever thou shall lose on earth shall be loosed in heaven." Matthew 16:13-19 (KJV)

This was the requirement that Christ was putting forth to His disciples to pass along to others, that, it was necessary for every man to know Jesus personally, as God who came in the flesh, according to the word of St John 1:1,14 **This is the path to salvation.** We must get this confession from all of the candidates for salvation before baptism. Each one must confess that Jesus is the only source of their salvation. Our faith in Jesus Christ is the beginning.

The path to salvation

No candidate is ready for baptism until he or she have made their confession of Christ in knowing who He is, and His work in redemption. That is, His death burial and resurrection. **We can't get back to God without a redeemer.**

In the New Testament book of Acts, we find that the eunuch had to believe on the name of Jesus, as both Lord and Christ before he could confess Christ's name, and be baptize in His name, as all others must also do.

Paul told the Jews what they must do:

"That if thou shall confess with thy mouth the Lord Jesus, and shall believe in thine heart that God hath raised Him from the dead, thou shall be saved." Romans 10:9 (KJV)

This does not say that you are saved, but this is a necessary step of the process too salvation, this is God's remedy for man's soul, these scriptures were the steps for the Eunuch. When the question was put to the eunuch; do you understand what you read? The response was, **how should I, except some man should guide me?** This is where hearing, believing and confessing the name of Jesus is applied. Then his understanding was opened concerning Christ, through the book of Isaiah 53.

The Message of Isaiah was this: the place of the Scriptures which he read was this,

"He was led as a sheep to the slaughter; and like a lamb dumb before His shearer, so opened He not His mouth: In His humiliation His judgment was taken away: and who shall declare His generation? For His life is taken from the earth." After the preaching of Isaiah 53:

"The Eunuch answered Philip, and said, I pray thee, of whom speaketh the prophet this? Of himself, or of some other man?

And Phillip opened his mouth, and began at the same Scripture, and preached unto him Jesus". (Acts 8:32-34 (KJV)

this is Isaiah's prophecy being spoken to the Eunuch in Acts eight, which was spoken in Isaiah fifty three.

"And as they went on their way, they came to a certain water: and the eunuch said, here is water; what do hinder me to be baptized?

And Phillip said, if thou believeth with all thine heart, thou mayest. And the Eunuch answered and said, I believe that Jesus Christ is the son of God. And he commanded the Chariot to stand still: and they went down both of them into the water, Phillip and the Eunuch; and he baptized him." Acts 8:36 – 38 (KJV)

Questions from the Author:

Have you set your husband at the head of your life, then God? 1st Corinthians 11:3

Reflection:

_____

_____

_____

_____

_____

_____

_____

_____

_____

_____

_____

_____

_____

_____

_____

_____

_____

_____

_____

_____

_____

CHAPTER III

Lessons Taught

The next principle in our salvation process is repentance.

Today, not much emphasis is put forth on repentance, as to say a sinners attitude must change, one must come to the end of self-realizing that he needs a positive change; and need to have a real desire to change and be saved from sin, to let go of sin, and to allow that natural spirit of a man to tell him if he's right or wrong. Today some ministers teach that repentance is not necessary, because Jesus took it all at Calvary; but there are many Scriptures on repentance, which calls all men everywhere to repent.

Let us see if repentance is still a requirement.

"Testifying both to the Jews, and also to the Greeks, repentance toward God, and faith toward our Lord Jesus Christ." Acts 20:21(KJV)

"And the times of this ignorance God winked at; but now commandeth all men everywhere to repent." Acts 17:30 (KJV)

If a person would consider in knowing right from wrong, and know that all sins that are committed is against God, and God alone. After David had sinned with Bathsheba, Uriah's wife; he said in his repentant prayer, **against thee only have I sinned.**

"Against thee, thee only, have I sinned, and done this evil in thy sight: that thou mightiest be justified when thou speaketh, and be clear when thou judges." Psalms 51:4 (KJV)

We trespass against men, but sin is always against God.

Even though David was a man after Gods own heart, he had to repent before God judged him while he was still in his sin.

Paul preached repentance to the gentiles

"...But shewed first unto them of Damascus. And at Jerusalem, and throughout all the coast of Judea, and then to the gentiles, that they should repent and turn to God, and do works meet for repentance." Acts 26:19-20 (KJV)

"Or despises thou the riches of His goodness and forbearance and longsuffering: not knowing that the goodness of God leadeth thee to repentance? For there is no respect of persons with God." Romans 2:4, 11 (KJV

Lesson taught continues

This actually is not the type of book that I would normally write. I feel that this type of writing is for a more sophisticated person; who might have a bit more flare on any subject. However, I dare to attempt to put my hand to this subject that I might bring a bit more clarity to some of the controversial subjects of today in a more simplified way, without the normal accusations, and maybe taking the sting out of the sins that we so easily participate in; opening our eyes in a quiet conversation.

Soon in this book we will begin to talk about lifestyles, genders and women in particular, please stay tuned.

However, if there be any doubt, or question in your mind about anything written in this document concerning our salvation, allow the Scriptures to guide you, that you may be redeemed through the word, and by the blood of the lamb. (Jesus) don't be lethargic about life and afraid to live it, it is great to be able to live without practicing sin every day, being free from fear, torment and controversy. Ask me I can tell you; because at one time that was my life: sin every day.

Thank God for life and salvation from the pull of sin, and the works of the devil. We must take responsibility for the wrong we've done, and the problems we've caused in doing so.

Sometimes maybe we should just sit down and in retrospect count all of the things that we know for sure that we've done wrong; and think about all the people we may have wounded with our lifestyle, our words and attitudes towards them. Consider other people's children that see our actions and attitude and how they want to pattern themselves after us. Think about how we are raising other people's children, and all other onlookers without realizing it, then we might say, is that really me? Oh how wrong I have been; Lord, please forgive me.

Wherefore, laying aside all malice, and all guile, and hypocrisies, and envies, and all evil speaking. As a new born babe, desire the sincere milk of the word that ye may grow thereby: If so be ye have tasted that the Lord is gracious. 1st Peter 2:1- 3 (KJV)

In our repentant state let our hearts convince us to put away evil, such as malice, having ill will toward another person. As Christ has forgiven you, you also must forgive others, According to the Scriptures.

I use the word "you" to make this very personal to those who may read it. We are commanded to put on a few things, as we put these things on, other things fall off. Praise the Lord!

As women we give life through child birth, and we do most of the daily teachings in life, and in schools. **As the so called weaker vessel,** our teaching must be sound at all times, because our teachings will cause the world to grow and prosper or crumble before our eyes in disgrace.

Promoting the spirit of Love.

"Love, the main ingredient Put *on therefore, as the elect of God, holy and beloved, bowels of mercies, kindness, humbleness of mind, meekness, longsuffering; forbearing one another, and forgiving one another, if any man have a quarrel against any: even as Christ forgave you, so also do ye.*

And above all these things put on charity, which is the bond of perfectness. And let the peace of God rule in your hearts, to the which also ye are called in one body; and be ye, thankful. Let the word of Christ dwell in you richly in all wisdom; teaching and admonishing one another in psalms and hymns and spiritual songs, singing with grace in your hearts to the Lord. And whatsoever you do in word or deed, do all in the name of the Lord Jesus, giving thanks to God the Father by Him." Colossians 3:12- 17 (KJV)

Remember what He said to do, put away: malice, guile, hypocrisies, envies, and all evil speaking.

"For if ye forgive men their trespasses, you're heavenly Father will also forgive you: But if you forgive not men their trespasses, neither will your Father forgive your trespasses." Matthew 6:14, 15 (KJV)

Repentance and sin; is an emotion which causes us to do things that we ought or ought not; so it is up to us to resist the devil, before and after our salvation.

*"**But He giveth more Grace**. Wherefore He saith, God resisteth the proud, but giveth grace unto the humble. Submit yourselves therefore to God. Resist the devil, and he will flee from you. Draw nigh to God, and He will draw nigh to you. Cleanse your hands, ye sinners; and purify your hearts, you double minded." James 4: 6-8 (KJV)*

After we have heard the word of God, concerning Jesus Christ: and His death burial and resurrection, and we also have believed the word which we've heard, and repented of all our sins, we might ask, what is the next step?

What do we do at this point, is there more? Did we do all that was required of us according to the Scriptures? I must say there is more to come.

The Process of Cleansing

How do we cleanse ourselves from that which we have already done and what is the process and what is the benefit of it in its totality? Thru repentance and the washing in water by baptism, applying the blood. We've heard of the baptism of the Eunuch; and how does that apply to us? It must be the same process and formula for every soul in this dispensation, God making no difference between us.

Paul said that there is no difference between the Jew and the Greek: the same Lord is over all. For whosoever shall call upon the name of the Lord shall be saved. Romans 10:12, 13 (KJV)

*"Then Peter said unto them, repent, and be baptized **every one** of you in the name of Jesus Christ for the remission of sins: and you shall receive the gift of the Holy Ghost." Acts 2:38 (KJV)* This power will cause us as women, not to continue to be that so called: weaker vessel.

Not only will you receive the gift of the Holy Ghost; according to the Scriptures, but you shall receive power, after that the Holy Ghost is come upon you. *Acts 1:8(KJV)*

"For the promise is unto you, and to your children, and to all that are a far off, even as many as the Lord our God shall call. Then they that gladly received his word were baptized: and the same day there were added unto them about three thousand souls. And they continued steadfastly in the apostle's doctrine and fellowship, and in breaking of bread, and in prayers. And fear came upon every soul: and many wonders and signs were done by the apostles." Acts 2:39-43(KJV)

The Questions was asked?

Why the people in the upper room of Acts 1:12-14 (KJV) was not baptized in water?

The answer to the question is: because this was a dispensation change from Old Testament to the New

Testament, and all the people of the previous dispensation had already met the requirements of baptism through John's baptism, so all they needed to do was to receive the Holy Ghost when Jesus sent it back after His resurrection. According to His promise to them, remember Jesus was talking to the Jews concerning this promise, and this is the Jewish nation we are speaking of, not the gentiles. St. John 14:15-18 (KJV)

This is why Jesus told them to tarry, (wait) in the city of Jerusalem until they were endued with power from on high, that they might receive the promise. Luke 24: 49(KJV) He gave them no other instruction concerning baptism. The three thousand souls that were baptized on the day of Pentecost; they were baptized in water and the Holy Ghost as were the hundred and twenty, having already met the requirements to receive the Holy Ghost through John's baptism.

"And, behold, I send the promise of my Father upon you: but tarry ye in the city of Jerusalem, until you be endued with power from on high." Luke 24:49 (KJV)

Because they had met the requirements to receive the Holy Ghost. Jesus told them to wait there and they would receive the Holy Ghost, to the Jew first; for it was His promise to them. On the day of Pentecost meaning fifty days after His death, burial and resurrection they all received the Holy Ghost, with the evidence of speaking in other tongues, as the Spirit gave them utterance, **without water baptism**.

"And when the day of Pentecost was fully come, they were all with one accord in one place. And suddenly there came a sound from heaven, as of a rushing mighty wind, and it filled all the house where they were sitting. And there appeared unto them, cloven tongues like as of fire, and it sat upon each of them. And they were all filled with the Holy Ghost, and began to speak with other tongues, as the Spirit gave them utterance." Acts 2:1- 4. (KJV)

Now we know this is to the Jewish church, to the Jew first, according to the Scriptures. There were one hundred and twenty names mentioned in the upper room but there were many dialects of languages there. Acts 2:5-12. (KJV)

*"For I am not ashamed of the gospel of Christ: for it is the power of God unto salvation to everyone that believeth; **to the Jew first**, and also to the Greek." Romans 1:16. (KJV)*

Identifying with Christ

So our next step to salvation would be: to be baptized in Jesus name for the remission of sins, with the promise of the Holy Ghost, identifying to the convert; that Christ is come into his or her temple. (Body) Baptism is a physical and spiritual requirement, which is commanded by God to be done for the remission of sins. It is very necessary to use the name of Jesus Christ in the formula of baptism. Through baptism a candidate is identified with Christ in His death, burial and resurrection. This is where we enter into relationship with Christ, in His burial. The counterpart of the water baptism is the spirit baptism. Both together equal the one baptism. As the Scriptures said "one Lord, one faith, one baptism.

"There is one body, one spirit, even as ye are called in one hope of your calling; One Lord, one faith, one baptism, One God and Father of all, who is above all, and through all, and in you all." Ephesians 4:4 – 6 (KJV)

The baptism which is the washing, the candidate can only be washed and cleansed when the blood is applied. How do we apply the blood? When the candidate goes into the water, the minister must speak the name of Jesus Christ over the candidate, while immersing him in water; then is the candidate buried with Jesus Christ in a watery grave, and rising up with Him from the grave in His resurrection from the dead, in newness of life.

This is the process, (the blood is the soap or cleansing agent which cleanses the sin when it is applied through Jesus' name. This baptism is the application and method of applying the blood). Remember, Father, son, and Holy Ghost are not names, only the attributes of God: the power is in the name, and that name is Jesus.

In the Name of Men

Remember, Noah's baptism and Moses baptism, it was unto Moses and in his name, which saith:

"Moreover, brethren, I would not that you should be ignorant, how that all our fathers were under the cloud, and all passed through the sea;

And were all baptized unto Moses *in the cloud and in the sea;"* 1ˢᵗ*Corinthians 10:1- 2 (KJV)*

"Christ also has once suffered for sins, the just for the unjust, that He might bring us to God, being put to death in the flesh, but quickened by the Spirit:

By which also He went and preached unto the spirits in prison;

Which sometime were disobedient, when once the long-suffering of God waited in the days of Noah, while the ark was a preparing, wherein few, that is, eight souls were saved by water.

The like figure whereunto even baptism do also now save us, "(not the putting away of the filth of the flesh, but the answer of a good conscience toward God), by the resurrection of Jesus Christ:" 1ˢᵗ *Peter 3:18-21 (KJV)*

Again we notice that all these people, Moses people, Noah's people, was saved thru water in a man's name. But when it comes to baptizing in Jesus dispensation, we hear Father, son, and Holy Ghost and not the man's name, Jesus. I challenge you to this thought, if Father, son, and Holy Ghost are names: then we must have three names or people. Why not consider?

Lesson Taught continue…

Our Baptism must be unto Jesus, that is, in His name.

Laying on of hands.

Laying on of the hands is the next possible step in receiving the Holy Ghost. If the candidate didn't receive the Holy Ghost immediately after their baptism, and if he or she is seriously seeking the Holy Ghost: The minister, or someone spiritual could or should lay their hands on the convert in the name of the Lord Jesus Christ, to cause them to be filled with the Holy Ghost.

Now when the apostles which were at Jerusalem heard that Samaria had received the word of God, they sent unto them Peter and John: Who, when they were come down, prayed for them, that they might receive the Holy Ghost: (For as yet He was fallen upon none of them: only they were baptized in the name of the Lord Jesus) Then laid they their hands on them, and they received the Holy Ghost… Acts 8:14-19(KJV)

Paul demonstrated the laying on of the hands, on twelve disciples, which had been baptized but had not received the Holy Ghost, this demonstrates to us that the Holy Ghost may not be given immediately after the baptism. So the candidate must seek after God for the Holy Ghost.

Jesus said that God gives the Holy Ghost to them that ask for it.

If you then, being evil, know how to give good gifts unto your children: how much more shall your heavenly Father give the Holy Spirit to them that ask Him? Luke 11:13 (KJV)

And we are His witnesses of these things; and so is also the Holy Ghost, whom God has given to them that obey Him." Acts 5:32 (KJV)

Peter calls for the obedience of repentance.

*"Then Peter said unto them, repent, and be baptized **every one** of you in the name of Jesus Christ for the remission of sins, and you shall receive the gift of the Holy Ghost." Acts 2:38 (KJV)*

It is imperative that we obey the Scriptures, if we are to receive salvation in its fulness as promised.

St. John's Gospel said: *"if ye ask anything in my name, I will do it. If you love me, keep my commandments. And I will pray the Father, and He shall give you another comforter that He may abide with you for ever; Even the Spirit of truth; whom the world cannot receive, because it seeth Him not, neither knoweth Him: but you know Him; for He dwelleth with you, and **shall be** in you." St. John 14: 14-18(KJV)*

Gentile's season

Now is the time of the gentiles, in Acts chapter 10. We find that the door is opened to the gentiles thru Peter's preaching, Cornelius being a gentile was commanded by an angel to send to Joppa for Peter to come and minister the word of God to the gentiles, (this was previously unheard of for it was against the law for a Jew to have contact with a gentile) though he would not be their future minister. But at this present time; Peter is the man that must put the seal of approval on the ministry as to whether or not all men received the Holy Ghost in the same manner with evidence of speaking in tongues. Why? Because Peter had the keys. That is, the revelation as to what and how this process must be done

"While Peter yet spake these words, the Holy Ghost fell on all them which heard the word. And they of the circumcision which believed were astonished, as many as came with Peter, because that on the gentiles also was poured out the gift of the Holy Ghost. For they heard them speak with tongues, and magnify God. Then answered Peter, Can any man forbid water, that these should not be baptized, which have received the Holy Ghost as well as we? And he commanded them to be baptized in the name of the Lord. Then prayed they him to tarry certain days." Acts 10: 44-48 (KJV)

Abraham's plea

This is how God felt about the sins of Sodom and Gomorrah, even the little cities in the plains, this is one episode in biblical history that we should never forget, and we should do everything in our power to prevent it from ever happening again. Think of God with the sadness in His heart for having to judge sin to this extreme. Think of the many souls that must have been lost because of unbelief: unbelief that their lifestyle was sin and they would be judge concerning it, these people were not judged for the sin of homosexuality alone, but mainly the sin of pride.

The scriptures said:

"Behold, this was the iniquity of Sodom, pride, fulness of bread, and abundance of idleness was in her and in her daughters, neither did she strengthen the hand of the poor and needy. And they were haughty, and committed abomination before me: therefore I took them away as I saw good." Ezekiel 16:49-50 (KJV) Their greatest sin was the sin of pride, as it is today.

"And the Lord said, because the cry of Sodom and Gomorrah is great, and because there sin is very grievous; I will go down now, and see whether they have done all together according to the cry of it, which is come unto me; and if not, I will know it.

And the men turned their faces from thence, and went toward Sodom: but Abraham stood yet before the Lord.

Here Abraham is pleading for the city and his nephew, Abraham knows that God will not hear him if he pleads for his nephew alone, so he pleads for the entire city even though he knows that God hates wickedness: then we find that the righteous judge knows very well how to judge righteously between good and evil, and will have compassion on the wicked; and spare them for the righteous sake.

And Abraham drew near, and said, wilt thou also destroy the righteous with the wicked? Peradventure there be fifty righteous in the city: wilt thou also destroy and not spare the place for the fifty righteous that are therein? That be far from thee to do after this manner, to slay the righteous with the wicked: and that the righteous should be as the wicked that be far from thee: shall the judge of all the earth do right? And the Lord said, if I find in Sodom fifty righteous within the city, then I will spare all the place for their sakes. And the Lord said, if I find in Sodom fifty righteous within the city, then I will spare all the place for their sakes.

Abraham's plea

And the Lord said, if I find in Sodom fifty righteous within the city, then I will spare all the place for their sakes.

And Abraham answered and said, behold now, I have taken upon me to speak unto the Lord, which am but dust and ashes: Peradventure there shall lack five of the fifty righteous: wilt thou destroy all the city for the lack of five? And He said, if I find there forty and five, I will not destroy it. And he spake unto him yet again, and said, peradventure there shall be forty found there. And He said I will not do it for forty's sake. And he said unto him, Oh let not the Lord be angry, and I will speak: peradventure there shall thirty be found there. And He said, I will not do it, if I find thirty there. And he said, behold now, I have taken upon me to speak unto the Lord: Peradventure there shall be twenty found there. And He said, I will not destroy it for twenty's sake and he said, Oh let not the Lord be angry, and I will speak but this once: peradventure ten shall be found there. And He said, I will not destroy it for ten's sake." Genesis 18:20 – 32(KJV)

Questions from the Author:

Did this book cause you to reflect on your past or current lifestyle? If so, what are your conclusions?

Reflection:

_____

_____

_____

_____

_____

_____

_____

_____

_____

_____

_____

_____

_____

_____

_____

_____

_____

_____

_____

_____

_____

CHAPTER IV

Is There a Triune God?

Before we really begin to talk about love let us talk about the triune God, and how this trinity works in God's plan of salvation for mankind. As we now know; God had all things in His mind before the world was. God put in place everything that was necessary for man's salvation. God always proves what is said by His word. When God needed a Redeemer for mankind: He looked for a man and found none; how do we apply the attributes of God as the trinity?

Discussing the Trinity of God

The trinity of God concerning our salvation is presented to us through the attributes of God.

"Remember, the scripture which saith: hear, O Israel: The LORD our God, is one Lord." Deuteronomy 6:4. (KJV)

God as Father ordained salvation. As we have discussed earlier. All things were done by God Himself, through Jesus Christ: His begotten son.

God as God; (Father an attribute of God) ordained our salvation that the world through Him might have eternal life before the foundation of the world.

God as Jesus, (son an attribute of God) purchased our salvation with His own precious blood at Calvary.

God as (Holy Ghost an attribute of God) applied it to our hearts.

This explains the trinity of God in each operations of His redemptive work for man.

"And the scriptures, foreseeing that God would justify the heathen through faith, preached before the gospel unto Abraham, saying, in thee shall all nations be blessed." Galatians 3:8 (KJV)

"Take heed therefore unto yourselves, and to all the flock, over the which the Holy Ghost hath made you overseers, to feed the church of God, which He hath purchased with His own blood." (Acts 20:28)

Note this

"To whom God would make known what is the riches of the glory of this mystery among the gentiles; which is Christ in you, the hope of glory." Colossians1:27 (KJV)

Discussing the trinity continue...

"According as He has chosen us in Him before the foundation of the world, that we should be holy and without blame before Him in love." God having the Gentiles in mind, before the foundation of the world." Ephesian 1:4

*"But we are bound to give thanks always to God for you, brethren beloved of the Lord, because **God has from the beginning chosen you to salvation through sanctification of the spirit and belief of the truth.***

Whereunto He called you by our gospel, to the obtaining of the glory of our Lord Jesus Christ." 2nd Thessalonian 2:13, 14 (KJV)

Our next thought Concerning the Trinity

As son or in the Sonship, He purchased salvation. He took upon Himself flesh and blood, and became a man. *"But when the fullness of the time was come God sent forth His son, made of a woman, under the law, to redeem them that were under the law, that we might receive the adoption of sons. And because ye are sons, God hath sent forth the spirit of His son into your hearts, crying, Abba, Father. "Galatian 4:4-6 (KJV)*

And this is the process in which He brought it to pass:

"In the beginning was the word, and the Word was with God, and the Word was God.

*And the Word was made flesh, and dwelt among us, (and we beheld **His glory**, the glory as of the only begotten of the Father,) full of grace and truth.*

***He** was in the world, and the world was **made by Him**, (not them, as Father, son and Holy Ghost, but as **by one. Him only**.) And the world **knew Him** not." John 1:1; 14, 10 (KJV)*

God Taking on the form of man

"Let this mind be in you, which was also in Christ Jesus: Who, being in the form of God, thought it not robbery to be equal with God: But made Himself of no reputation, and took upon Him the form of a servant, and was made in the likeness of men: And being found in fashion as a man, He humbled Himself, and became obedient unto death, even the death of the cross.

Wherefore God also has highly exalted Him, and given Him a name which is above every name." *Philippians 2:5-9. (KJV)*

"This name is above the name of every power or principality known. Above death, Satan, sickness, addictions of every kind, and all evil and wicked spirits. This name is Jesus.

Our third part of the Trinity of God's attributes.

Scriptures to understand for assurance

As the Holy Ghost, He applied salvation to the heart of the believer."

And I will pray the Father, and He shall give you another comforter, that He may abide with you forever: Even the Spirit of truth; whom the world cannot receive, because it seeth Him not, neither knoweth Him: but you know Him; for He dwelleth with you, and shall be in you. I will not leave you comfortless; I will come to you." St. John 14:16-18 (KJV)

"But, ye are not in the flesh, but in the spirit, if so be that the spirit of God dwell in you. Now if any man have not the spirit of Christ, he is none of His. Romans 8:9 (KJV)

And because ye are sons, God has sent forth the Spirit of His son unto your hearts, crying, Abba, meaning Father." Galatians 4:6 (KJV)

"There is one body, and one spirit, even as you are called in one hope of your calling; One Lord, one faith, one baptism, ***One God and Father of all****, who is above all, and through all, and in you all." Ephesians 4:4-6 (KJV)*

"According as He hath chosen us in Him before the foundation of the world, that we should be holy and without blame before Him in love: Having predestinated us unto the adoption of children by Jesus Christ to Himself, according to the good pleasure of His will. To the praise of the glory of His

grace, wherein He hath made us accepted in the beloved."
Ephesians 1:4-6 (KJV)

Document the name

In order to call Jesus, God, Son, and or Holy Ghost: we must search the Scriptures to know if, Jesus is God or if Jesus is Son, or if He is the Holy Ghost.

The Third Part of the Trinity of the Attributes of God

Note this

These scriptures are for the people who can't believe that Jesus is God Himself, or that He is come in the flesh. Thomas called Him, his Lord and God.

…And Thomas answered and said unto Him, my Lord and my God. St John 20:19-20 (KJV)

THESE SCRIPTURES SAITH THAT JESUS IS THE TRUE GOD, AND ETERNAL LIFE.

"And we know that the son of God is come, and has given us an understanding, that we may know Him that is true, and we are in Him that is true, even in His son Jesus Christ. This is the true God, and eternal life." 1ˢᵗ John 5:20 (KJV)

"Hereby know you the Spirit of God: every spirit that confesses that Jesus Christ is come in the flesh is of God: meaning. Jehovah the Savior." 1ˢᵗ John 4:2(KJV)

"And this is life eternal, that they might know thee the only true God, Jesus Christ whom thou hath sent."
St John 17:3 (KJV)

Only the scriptures are true, not our denominational doctrines or our own personal beliefs. We must consult the Old and the New Testament for a complete understanding of the word. (Isaiah 34:16) tells us that every scripture has a back-up scripture for support and understanding;

"Whatsoever things were written aforetime was written for our learning... let us consult and believe the scriptures."
Romans 15:4 (KJV)

The Ordinances of the Church

Things a new convert must practice. Because he or she is new in the faith, and have no strength in the Lord, like Eve to stand before the devil, it is imperative that the new converts attend all biblical classes, and studies that he or she may begin to have biblical knowledge and understanding of the Scriptures as a Christian. This is, that, he or she may learn the customs and doctrines of the church. Hebrew warns us to participate by saying,

"Not forsaking the assembling of yourselves together as the manner of some is; but exhorting one another: and so much the more, as you see the Day approaching." Hebrews 10:25(KJV)

Again, it is said, "Be followers of me, even as I also am of Christ. Now I praise you, brethren, that ye remember me and all things, and keep the ordinances, as I have delivered them to you." 1St. Corinthians 11:1, 2. (KJV)

What is ordinances, question number one?

This tells us why we should be present in all the church services; this tells us that there are many things which we must begin to learn, know and understand, just as the world has their own language so does the church. This is just one more thing that must be learned. All professions have their own language that whosoever is a part of that profession must learn. It is mandatory to learn the language or you will lack understanding, and so does the church.

Ordinances are traditions: A custom or practice handed down by predecessors, or from one generation to the next. These traditions set forth for the church in the area of public tradition in the context of the above Scripture, a woman was to always be in subjection to her own husband.

"But I would have you know, that the head of every man is Christ; and the head of the woman is the man; and the head of Christ is God." 1ˢᵗ Corinthians 11:2 (KJV)

This is prompting the idea that certain customs or traditions are not relevant for us in the new day, or in the future. However, it is still required of us as saints, to present ourselves as saints in our attire, and not as one for soliciting special attention, nor favors from people for positions or sexual favours.

Not to offend: along with other areas where we are not to offend is; especially to the new convert; for they are babes in Christ, fragile and sensitive, and easily wounded. We are never to frustrate the new people that are trying to come out of the world, and into the church body before they know how to withstand criticism from religious saints, which so quickly becomes the enemy in their eyes.

Offense would be the main thing to drive them from the church before they have an opportunity to know

Christ. It is imperative that we must be sensitive in all that we teach and especially in our walk with Christ, because we are the first living letters which they will read.

"You are our epistle written in our hearts, known and read of all men." 2ⁿᵈ Corinthians 3:2. (KJV)

How not to offend

Never present to a person anything that you know offends them, whether it be religion, food, clothing, or makeup, or even jewelry. Though it is impossible not to offend some, but the point is, not to offend knowingly. This is part of the Christian walk.

"It is reported commonly among you that there is fornication among you, and such fornication is not so much as named among the Gentiles, that one should have his father's wife." 1ˢᵗ Corinthians 5:1 (KJV)

The unsaved are especially vulnerable. Open worldly pleasures in the church disrespects the church body of Christ. This causes sinners not to come into the body and new saints to distrust the church as a whole. It is not wise to offend the unsaved such as the violation of other people's rights.

The Church of God

It is personally and highly recommended, that you never leave the place of service where you are visiting; or temporarily attending in order to go to your home church, or another church service, remember that all church doors belong to God, and God currently has you where he wants you to be at present by his spirit: and not by tradition of religion.

There is a number of things that we must learn as new saints, and as Christians, and as obedient children of God.

1. We must learn to tithe, tithing is not an automatic process, it is something we must learn to do willingly; our hearts are grudgingly creatures, and tight towards the church, and we must learn to give to God that which is His freely: the church, and the people of God for many reasons. (We give generously at worldly events without question, why not do the same in the house of God?

We are told that what we earn belongs to us, but we forget about the government and what they consider to be their share. The city and state exact from our checks automatically, we pay all the bills for that city. Parks, hospitals, schools, roads, municipalities utilities, and all that the city and state think they have need of, yet, we have an issue with giving to the church of God as little as a tithe. A tithe is as little as a tenth of your earnings according to the preacher; but I would say the tithe is a tenth of your increase, that is, your net, because the gross never came to you, it never belonged to you just as the tithe never belonged to you it is God's part.

2. Tithing is not only money, but is also of your time, talent and your effort. There are scriptures concerning tithing, in the Old Testament and the New Testament.

This is the blessing of the tithe

"The question is asked, will a man robbed God? Yet you have robbed me. But ye say, wherein have we robbed thee? In tithes and offerings.

Ye are cursed with a curse: for ye have robbed me, even this whole nation.

Bring ye all the tithes into the storehouse, that there may be meet in mine house, and prove me now herewith, saith the Lord of host, if I will not open you the windows of heaven, and pour you out a blessing, that there shall not be room enough to receive it. And I will rebuke the devourer for your sakes, and he shall not destroy the fruits of your ground; neither shall your vines cast her fruit before the time in the field, says the Lord of host.

And all nations shall call you blessed: for ye shall be a delightsome land, says the Lord of host." Malachi 3:6-12(KJV)

"Thou shall not delay to offer the first of thy ripe fruits, and of thy liquors: the first born of thy sons shall they give unto me." Exodus 22:29 (KJV)

"For this Melchisedec, king of Salem, priest of the most high God, who met Abraham returning from the slaughter

of the kings, and blessed him; to whom also Abraham gave a tenth part of all; first being by interpretation, king of righteousness, and after that also king of Salem, which is, king of peace; without Father, without Mother, without dissent, having neither beginning of days, nor end-of-life; but made like unto the son of God; abided a priest continually.

Now consider how great this man was, unto whom even the patriarch Abraham gave the tenth of the spoils. And verily they that are of the sons of Levi, who received the office of the priesthood, have a commandment to take tithes of the people, according to the law, that is, of their brethren, though they come out of the loins of Abraham: But He whose dissent is not counted from them received tithes of Abraham, and blessed Him that had the promises. And without all contradiction. The less is blessed of the better. And here men that die receive tithes; but there he received them, of whom it is witness that He liveth. And as I may so say, Levi also, who receiveth tithes, payed tithes in Abraham. For he was yet in the loins of his father, when Melchisedec met him; Hebrew 7:1-9." (Matthew 23:23KJV)

You must be asking the question: what does all of this have to do with salvation and Christianity?

A. It show's our obedience to the word, and our duty to God's work.

B. This is how the church supports the things of God, and the house of God.

C. This supports the preacher, and all who live by the gospel

Questions to consider

"*Who goeth warfare any time at his own charges? Who planteth a vineyard, and eateth not of the fruit thereof? Or who feedeth a flock, and eateth not of the milk of the flock? Say me these things as a man? Or saith not the law the same also? For it is written in the Law of Moses, thou shall not muzzle the mouth of the ox that treadeth out the corn. Doth God take care for oxen? Or saith He it all together for our sakes? For our sakes, no doubt, this is written: that he that ploweth should plow in hope; and that he that threshes in hope should be partakers of his hope. If we have sown unto you spiritual things, is it a great thing if we shall reap off your cardinal things? Do you not know that they which minister about holy things live of the things of the temple? And they which wait at the altar are partakers with the altar?*

Even so hath the **Lord ordained that they which preach the gospel should live of the gospel**.*"* 1st Corinthians 9: 7- 14(KJV)

"*And, behold, I have given the children of Levi all the tenth in Israel for an inheritance, for their service which they serve, even the service of the Tabernacle of the congregation. Thus speak unto the Levites, and say unto them, when you take of the children of Israel the tithes which I have given you from them for your inheritance, then you shall offer up an heave offering of it for the Lord, even a tenth part of the tithe." Numbers 18:21, 26, 28. (KJV)*

"Thus ye also shall offer an heave offering unto the Lord of all your tithes, which ye shall receive of the children of Israel; and you shall give thereof all of the Lord's heave offering to Aaron the priest;" Numbers 18:28(KJV)

We are taught that if we should miss bringing our tithe to the church, that we should make it up the next time we come to church, the tithe is brought not paid: that is the Lord's part that we bring. It is not a debt which we owe it belongs to Him. The giving of our offerings is freewill in its' amount; for other reasons such as building fund is also required as well, there is an offering called the poor saints offering also.

"And the Lord Spake unto Moses, saying, Speak to the children of Israel, that they bring me an offering: of every man that giveth it willingly, with his heart ye shall take my offering." Exodus 25:1, 2(KJV

Old Testament Principles Brought Forth

"Now concerning the collection for the saints, as I have given order to the churches of Galatia, even so do ye." 1st Corinthians 16:1(KJV)

"I have showed you all things, how that so laboring ye ought to support the weak, and to remember the words of

the Lord Jesus, how he said, it is more blessed to give than to receive." Acts 20: 35. (KJV)

Dress and Attire

The custom of dress and of our costumes must be addressed in the new convert's life. Our dress sometimes identifies us as in our profession; when we see a judge in his robe, we're pretty sure that's the judge, when we see a person pushing the cart in the hotel, we assume he or she is a maid, or a porter. So our attire identifies us to the average person, whether it be high-class, moderate dress, tattered dress, and so on; we identify the person with what they are wearing.

We can know if they're rich, poor, middle class, or homeless. Even male or female simply by their attire, so it is important as Christians to be identified as such, not as anything else, or anyone else but that which becometh saints.

God decking His people

The Scripture does say: that there was a time when God saw Israel, and Israel was not enticing, but polluted, and He took her and cleaned her up, and made her beautiful. So this tells us that God believes in beauty and jewelry. Though we have men who refuse to allow some women in the church to wear jewelry at all nor any makeup on their face this is not an ordinance of God, but a tradition of men, because of their own personal thoughts: you can draw your own conclusion on this one.

"*And say, thus saith the Lord God unto Jerusalem; thy birth and thy nativity are of the land of Canaan; thy father was an Amorite, and thy mother and Hittite. And as for thy nativity, and the day that thou wast born thy navel was not cut, neither was thou washed in water to supple thee; thou wast not salted at all, nor swaddled at all.*

None eye pitied thee, to do any of these unto thee, to have compassion upon thee; but thou wast cast out in the open field, to the loathing of thy person, in the day that thou wast born.

And when I passed by thee, and saw thee polluted in thine own blood, I said unto thee when thou wast in thy blood, Live; yea, I said unto thee, when thou wast in thy blood, Live.

I have caused thee to multiply as the bud of the field, and thou hast increased and waxen great, and thou art come to excellent ornaments: thy breast or fashioned, and thine hair is grown, whereas thou wast naked and bare. Now when I passed by thee, behold, thy time was the time of love; and I spread my skirt over thee yea, and covered thy nakedness. Yea, I swear unto thee, and entered into a covenant with thee, saith the Lord God, and thou becameth mine.

Then washed I thee with water; yea, I thoroughly washed away thy blood from thee, and I anointed thee with oil.

God decking His people continues

I clothe thee also with broidered work, and shod thee with badgers' skin, and I girded thee about with fine linen, and I cover thee with silk. I decked thee also with ornaments, and I put bracelets upon thy hands, and a chain on thy neck. And I put a jewel on thy forehead, and earrings in thine ears, and a beautiful crown upon thine head.

Thus was thou decked with gold and silver; and thy raiment was of fine linen, and silk, and broidered work; thou didst eat fine flour, and honey, and oil; and thou was exceeding beautiful, and thou didst prosper into a kingdom.

And by renowned went forth among the heathen for thy beauty: for it was perfect through my comeliness, which I had put up on thee, saith the Lord God. But thou didst trust in thine own beauty, and playedst the harlot because of thy renowned, and pouredst out thy fornication on everyone that passed by: his it was." Ezekiel 16:3 – 15. (KJV)

This is a bad example of things represented as the woman: the weaker vessel

This is a great example of attire, beauty, and cleanliness. When we're not quite so beautiful, or attractive, we don't get much attention, but when we adorn ourselves improperly; we may very well attract the wrong type of attention.

It is most important to know how to dress, as saints, representing Christ.

I must say that clothes very well enhances a person's beauty, so does our hair and a few other things about the body, even though God loves the beauty of the female, as the church. He also has a standard for both; there should also be a distinction between the things of the male and the things of the female, as God has made us distinctively different, male and female. As male and female, the male should remain with that which pertaineth to the male, and the female should remain with that which pertaining to the female, no shame in this.

Things new converts should know:

When ideas change about certain things, the intent is to also change the design and traditions of the things of old, calling them out of date; believe me somethings should never change.

God Decking His People

Yes, traditions, cultures, and costumes change but Jesus is the same yesterday, today and forever more.

A difference must always be maintained to reflect the distinction between the male and the female. God in the beginning made them both male and female. This will never be changed! And let us never forget that fact, and hold to the ways of God.

Questions from the Author:

After reflecting on what you have read; how can you be better prepared for life as a woman?

Reflection:

_____

_____

_____

_____

_____

_____

_____

_____

_____

_____

_____

_____

_____

_____

_____

_____

_____

_____

_____

_____

_____

CHAPTER V

Gender difference

In our thoughts about homosexuality: first let us determine what God did.

In God's creation, God created the male and the female only. (Genesis 1:28 KJV) no other gender did He create, nor did He suggest that another gender or lifestyle should be presented in the future. He did not create what people call homosexuals nor Lesbians,

The words homosexual and lesbians are verbs, this is a sexual action which is performed between same sex couples prayerfully behind closed doors; in private as all sexual acts should be performed. God did not create verbs as people, He created nouns as people; so in reality homosexuals do not exist as people, only the act of the word exists.

Is there such a thing as Gay people? Yes! Only, if, they are: brightly colored or showy, merry, excited, full of joy and fun, given to lightheartedness, Example: they lead a gay life, free from responsibility and worry.

Not the performance of a sexual act, homosexually or otherwise. The word homosexual is described as an act which is performed between same sex couples.

Did God say that He hated Homosexuals? NO! He did not.

He did not give the people the name homosexual, He named the act of that unlawful sex as an abomination: However, He did plainly say that the act of such is abomination to Him, and those that do such things is worthy of death.

"Thou shalt not lie with mankind, as with womankind: it is abomination. Meaning (Unclean, vile affections, against nature.)" Leviticus 18:22 (KJV)

"If a man also lie with mankind, as he lieth with a woman, both of them have committed an abomination: they shall be put to death; their blood shall be upon them." Leviticus 20:13 (KJV)

It is the act of un-natural sex which God hates, not people. Everything is forgivable with God, if a person repents and turns from his un-Godly ways.

Note

Sin is outside of salvation: it is evil and of the devil. In this case salvation must be sought with a sincere repentant heart, to obtain mercy and forgiveness, thru the blood of

Jesus Christ, with the washing of water in baptism in His name; and the name is Jesus, not Father, Son and Holy Ghost.

Wherefore save yourselves, turn to God's natural prescribed way in all sexual activity.

"Wherefore God also gave them up to uncleanness through the lust of their own hearts, to dishonor their own bodies between themselves.

For this cause God gave them up unto vile affections: ***for even their women*** *did change the natural use into that which is against nature.*

And likewise also the men, leaving the natural use of the woman, burned in their lust one toward; another, men with men working that which is unseemly, and receiving in themselves that recompense of their error which is meet." *Romans 1:24, 26-27.*

Words to the disobedient

"Knowing this, that the law is not made for a righteous man, but for the lawless and disobedient, ***for the ungodly, and for sinners, for unholy and profane, for murderers of fathers and murderers of mothers, for manslayers,***

For whoremongers, ***for them that defile themselves with mankind, for menstealers, for liars, for perjured persons,*** *and if there be any other thing that is contrary to* sound doctrine." *1st. Timothy 1:9,10 (KJV) read this first, the entire Chapter of Romans.*

Jesus asked the question: "and why call ye me, Lord, Lord, and do not the things which I say?" Luke 6:46(KJV)

This plainly shows us that God is not judging people who call themselves homosexuals only, but all sinners who refuse to repent.

LGBT

LGBT is another lifestyle that should be addressed with the new convert; having them to understand gender differences, and what God's purpose was for the male and for the female body, according to the Scriptures. It was, and still is, to multiply and to replenish the earth: with the sexual pleasures added. Any person having a desire to become a member in the body of Christ must learn what Christ expects of that person.

Yes, Jesus loves all the people, but there is a price to be paid for sin and disobedience.

"And God blessed them, and God said unto them, be fruitful, and multiply, and replenish the earth, and subdue it: and have dominion…" Gen. 1:28 (KJV)

"The wages of sin is death; but the gift of God is eternal life through Jesus Christ our Lord." Romans 6:23 (KJV)

"For if we sin willfully after that we have received the knowledge of the truth, there remaineth no more sacrifice for sin." Hebrews 10:26 (KJV) According to the scripture.

Males produce, females conceive: even the butterfly.

We all must learn what constitutes a male, and what constitutes a female, these studies should be in individual groups, because these are special services offered as part of the teachings to body of Christ, and some people may have stories to tell concerning themselves that other ears; or all of the body should not be privileged to hear at that time; that's why they would be called specials.

This new society of open gender difference has caused our biblical teaching to intensify in knowledge concerning Christian living. These are my own personal thoughts, which I believe is backed-up by the scriptures.

Disclaimer:

No man taught me these truths on this particular subject, thus I received them from the Holy Spirit.

To the T's: doctors should counsel a person that chooses to change their gender, because of the desires of the heart; a male that wishes to become a female should have the understanding of What constitutes a female; before the idea of a sex change is even fully formed in his mind.

Number one question that should be asked by the doctor to the male is, do you have a womb to bare children? And, can you give natural suck to an infant? (The breast)

Number Two question should be: Have you already reproduced yourself from your own seed? These questions opens up the proper type of dialogue concerning this process, and the thoughts of the heart. This is the beginning of understanding and wisdom concerning lifestyles changes.

Just to speak to the T's. No offence please

A male that wishes to become a woman, such as a news worthy malefactor did, (and yes, He is still a male because of creation, whether he likes it or not;) or the likes thereof should understand who they are: first by creation, if the male can, and, or may have already reproduced himself through his seed: like this man did; this is what constitutes the male.

The male of every flower, every tree, every insect, every dog or cat, the monkey, the elephant, the fish, the birds and such like, which reproduces himself through his seed is the male. Remember, the male has no womb to bare, nor can he reproduce himself through the bearing of the fruit of the womb; (children) he produces the seed to bring forth that life. (Children being called fruit of the womb) This is a subject that should be addressed by Holy Ghost filled clergy and not Lay professionals, because of their possible lack of biblical knowledge in this subject.

As for the female:

The description for the female: is that she has a womb to bear children whether her womb is shut up or not, or whether she choose to bare are not, and she also has paps to give suck to an infant. The female has no seed to reproduce herself as does the male. The seed always comes from the male, even in the lavatory and this is the way nature wrote the script through God's wisdom and knowledge, nothing added.

Any changes that are made outside of the natural use of the body is due to our own desires, and other spirits which may have invaded; or is attacking our physiological thinking.

Biblical truths

This is why we need Holy Ghost filled ministers to address the issue with the person; this is where God needs to be involved in this process for guidance, and instruction to a mind and heart which may be in turmoil, and stress.

"The words of God are spirit and life. It is the spirit that quickeneth; the flesh profiteth nothing: the words that I speak unto you, they are Spirit, and life." St. John 6:63 (KJV)

"And I will visit upon her, the days of Baalim, wherein she burned incense to them, and decked herself with her earrings and her jewels, and she went after her lovers, and forgat me, saith the Lord." Hosea 2:13(KJV)

The Bible warns against the excessiveness of ornaments and requires that our clothing and ornaments be worn as modest apparel, we are not to be flamboyant as some.

"In like manner also, that women adorn themselves in modest apparel, with shamefacedness and sobriety; not with braided hair, or gold, or pearls, or costly array;

But (which become the women professing godliness) with good works." 1ˢᵗ Timothy 2:9,10(KJV)

Again

"Knowing this, that the law is not for a righteous man, but for the lawless and disobedient, for the ungodly and for

sinners, for unholy and profane, for murders of fathers and mothers, for manslayers,

*For whoremongers, **for them that defile themselves with mankind**, for menstealers, for liars, for perjured persons, and if there be any other thing that is contrary to sound doctrine.*

According to the glorious gospel of the blessed God which was committed to my trust;" 1st. Timothy 1:9-11. (KJV)

Ornaments and or jewelry, sexual sins of homosexuality, fornication, Adultery, oral sex, murder, liars, thieves, haters of the brethren and such like, does not constitute the Christian lifestyle. Society say these pleasures are good and normal, but the scriptures say they are outside of the Christian lifestyle. Unclean and unholy.

Don't be offended, simply make the corrections while there is life in the body.

Speaking to the woman

Question: Dose Satan still speak to the woman as the weaker vessel for immoral change as he did to Eve in the garden? He spoke to Eve, not to Adam; to bring moral destruction into the home. However, as the priest of his house the male chose not to stand up to the spirit of Satan to save or defend his house from destruction when evil came to him through the voice of his wife;

"And **the serpent said unto the woman**, *ye shall not surely die:*

For God doth know that in the day ye eat thereof, then your eyes shall be opened, and ye shall be as gods, knowing good and evil.

*And **when the woman saw** that the tree was good for food, and that it was pleasant to the eyes, and a tree to be desired to make one wise, she took of the fruit thereof, and did eat, and **gave also unto her husband with her; and he die eat**.*" *Genesis 3:4-6(KJV)*

(This is Deception being used on the female, while the husband looked on, and heard and did nothing, as they do unto this day.)

"**And unto Adam He said, because though hast hearkened unto the voice of thy wife. And hast eaten of the tree, of which I commanded thee, saying, thou shall not eat of it:** *cursed is the ground for thy sake; in sorrow shalt thou eat of it all the days of thy life;*" *Genesis 3: 17 (KJV)*

This is the result of Adams disobedience, and him hearkening to the voice of his wife. There is always a horrific price to pay for sin.

Then there was Sarah:

*"Now Sarai Abram's wife bare him no children: and she had a handmaid, an Egyptian, whose name was Hagar. And **Sarai said** unto Abram, behold now, the LORD hath restrained me from bearing: I pray thee, **go in unto my maid;** it may be that I may obtain children by her. **And Abram hearkened to the voice of his wife.**" Genesis 16:1-2 (KJV)*

And like Adam hearkening to the voice of his wife, and Abram doing the same thing with his wife Sarai, it seems that Satan always approaches the woman for these changes, and the world is paying a heavy price of suffering and death for the pleasures of their flesh unto this day. Simply because the man wouldn't stand up to the spirit of Satan in his own home, him, the man, loving the thrills of his flesh, and being able to partake of the forbidden fruit chose death and destruction for all.

Again, the woman **(wife)** rose up and spoke to her husband to go against the will of the LORD, but this time we found a man (Christ-like) who stood-up to the spirit of Satan that was coming against his house, of course he suffered for it, (as a prologue like Christ did at Calvary). Him like any others that stands up for righteousness, but he rebuked his wife and stayed in the position of the priest of his own house, and was in line for his house to be regenerated in God's timing. **This man did not harken to the voice of his wife**: This man is named JOB.

"And the Lord said unto Satan, Behold, all that he hath is in thy power; only upon himself put not forth thine hand." Job 1:12 (KJV)

"And the Lord said unto Satan, Behold, he is in thine hand; but save his life. So went Satan forth from the presence of the LORD, and smote JOB with sore boils from the sole of his foot unto his crown.

And he took him a potsherd to scrape himself withal; and he sat down among the ashes.

Then said his wife unto him, dost thou still retain thine integrity? Curse God, and die.

Job abruptly rebuked his wife by saying to her:

But he said unto her, thou speaketh as one of the foolish women speaketh. What? Shall we receive good at the hand of God, and shall we not receive evil? In all this did not Job sin with his lips." Job 2:6-10 (KJV)

Old Testament sin carried over into the New Testament life:

Again we see the woman being listed first: as the one bringing the moral decline into society; by changing the natural use of God's plan for the body. As we have seen through Eve and Sarah and Job's wife; Satan seems to mostly approach the woman with the voice of moral corruption with the man being aware, but in silence.

If you notice in today's LGBT community the female is mentioned first.

In the book of Romans the females are mentioned first, so this might say to some; that this is why a woman should not be the first in leadership, because as it was previously stated that it was the woman that was deceived not the man. 1ˢᵗ Timothy 2:14 (KJV)

"For Adam was first formed, then Eve. And Adam was not deceived, but the woman being deceived was in the transgression." 1ˢᵗ Timothy 2:13, 14 (KJV)

She broke God's law while the man stood by without protest, as for the man: as the priest of the house or preachers, again, the males are silent

Chosen for Greatness

"Just as God has chosen the woman for greatness; the devil had chosen her also as a weapon to be used against God, through the family lifestyle and the church.

For I am jealous over you with Godly jealously; for I have espoused you to one husband, that I may present you as a chaste virgin to Christ. But I fear, lest by any means, as the Serpent beguiled Eve through his subtility, so your minds should be corrupted from the simplicity that is in Christ." 2ⁿᵈ Corinthians 11:2,3 (KJV)

A word to the LGBT and the general populace

Let us make some corrections in our identification of some people. Let me first say that there is no such person as a homosexual: Everything always goes back to creation and the scriptures; whether we believe it or not. In the beginning God created mankind as male and female only, with nothing added.

Question: when did any other species of humans come upon the face of the earth?

Again, God created the male and the female only, He never called any man a homosexual, nor did He call the woman a lesbian, He named them human names, the man He called Adam, and the woman He called Eve. He did however, say; that, same gender sexual acts which some of His humans performed between themselves was an abomination unto Him. (Meaning unclean, filthy, against the law of Nature.)

In the general dictionary, the word abomination (Meaning that the act which is an abomination to God is: 1. disgusting, or loathing; detestable action or practice. 2. Intense disgust, hatred, or loathing)

So it is the action which the same sex couples perform that God hates, and not the people: His love for mankind is universal, and this is why there is forgiveness for such crimes against God, and the sins of the human body. God's forgiveness is the place of salvation, and deliverance for the soul from everlasting destruction should anyone repent. Remember! **Jesus paid the price for all sin,** even though the price was His death, while we were yet sinners, He paid our sin debt. **Why should we die for a debt that's already paid?**

Hear This:

"Whom God hath set forth to be a propitiation through faith in His blood, to declare His righteousness for the remission of sins that are past, through the forbearance of God." Romans 3:25(KJV)

"For God commendeth His love toward us, in that, while we were yet sinners, Christ died for us. Much more then, being now justified by his blood, we shall be saved from wrath through Him." Romans 5:8, 9 (KJV)

LGBT Truths Revealed

It seems that the female doesn't recognize her creator as having a special place for her in His creation or society, and that she is on the outside as man, and Satan would have her to be, so she thinks she can do as she pleases in her behavioral rebellion in such practices. However, the scriptures said that He was jealous over the woman, the reason for this is? Because He, God that is, wants her to be adorned as a peculiar bride unto Himself as His church. This is why Satan makes his approach to the woman instead of the man, to pollute the woman means to abort the church, and to destroy the plan of salvation.

Satan seeks to keep her (the church or woman) spoiled and unclean before God, imperfect, unholy; to abort her as Christs' bride (the church). No sex involved in this relationship, but pure undefiled intimacy between God and the woman as being in covenant relationship with Him as His adorned bride: the church. Women are more adored by God than they or the world might imagine. God's church must be spotless, holy and righteous as He is righteous.

Check this out, again

"For I am jealous over you with godly jealousy: ***for I have espoused you to one husband****, (husband means: **male***) that I may present you as a chaste virgin to Christ. But I fear, lest by any means, as the serpent beguiled Eve through his subtility, so your minds should be corrupted from the simplicity that is in Christ." 2nd Corinthians 11:2-3 (KJV)*

LGBT did you notice?

Did you notice that the females were named first as the one who went away from the natural use of the man, or the body? Let us look at what's been said about us as women.

First, let's talk about society as a whole, the scriptures have given us a command not to have any fellowship with the **unfruitful works of darkness, the LGBT community produces no fruit as God planned it from the beginning in multiplying fruit from the womb.**

The male and the female becoming one through the sexual intercourse, the baby being one of them, or one in them. So we are accused by some in our society, as well as by the LGBT community as being prejudice against them. However, the saints as sons and daughters of God must obey that which their Father has spoken unto them, and not their emotions fleshly cravings and desires.

To the LGBT and the general populace

If the LGBT community chooses to see it another way, and refuse to receive Gods law as it is written in the scriptures, then the blood is on their own heads, but as they choose to believe their way; they must also allow others to believe as they have chosen to believe without prejudice from the LGBT community. Just as no one in America has made a law to incarcerate any LGBT's for disobeying what we may consider to be breaking God's law: there should not be a law against others who disagree with their lifestyle as law.

The price for sin according to God's law is too great, sexual or otherwise: it will cost a person total separation from God... According to the scriptures.

Judgement noted

"He that overcometh shall inherit all things; and I will be his God, and he shall be my son.

But the fearful, and unbelieving, and the abominable, and murderers, and whoremongers, and sorcerers, and idolaters, and all liars, shall have their part in the lake which burneth with FIRE and BRIMSTONE: which is the second death." Revelation 21:7, 8 (KJV)

This is for non-repentant sinners. Minister's only try to warn, and inform the world of impending everlasting punishment to none repentant sinners. Maybe we are not subtle enough like Satan in our approach.

LGBT's say that others are prejudice against them, but LGBT's are also prejudice against others when they pass a law against others right to freedom of speech; which say "other people must agree with how they live," the bottom line is: LGBT "crush other people rights in pride" if they have the nerve to think or have and opinion about a certain lifestyle, while LGBT make laws which say they can have it both ways.

What LGBT is saying is: that they will deny everyone else their rights in order to establish their own, but it will always be other people in their perception that are prejudice and not them. Wow! Perfect sinners.

Note

The scripture said"

"Proving what is acceptable unto the Lord. And having no fellowship with the unfruitful works of darkness, but rather reprove them. For it is a shame even to speak of those things which are done of them in secret." Ephesians 5: 10-12 (KJV)

God said to the male and the female to multiply and replenish the earth.

"And God blessed them, and God said. Unto them, be fruitful, and multiply, and replenish the earth, and subdue it: and have dominion over the fish of the sea, and over the fowl of the air, and over every living thing that moveth upon the earth." Genesis 1:28 (KJV)

A view of the female, then the male

A Subliminal Message

There is no fruit between same sex couples, but, they covet other people's children in order to create a family, so this alone tells the world that they believe in family as God had said, (*be fruitful and multiply*) but at some place along the way they have aborted the plan of God in the natural process of producing the

family in their lives: through lust, and passion toward one another.

A view of the female

Let us look at what is being said about the female and then the male. No mention of B.T (bisexual or transgendered) apparently they were not to be so in the mind of God. It seems that they have created something new for themselves as Satan has infiltrated their minds to change God's law concerning the body, as he did Eve in the garden in the partaking of the tree of good and evil, instead of the tree of life: aborting God's future sons, bringing them down to eternal death through sin.

Remember, it was the woman that was deceived by the serpent, not the man. This is because Satan was never after the man, so the man never contented with Satan, as did the woman.

"For Adam was formed first, then Eve. And Adam was not deceived, but the woman being deceived was in the transgression." (Meaning, she broke God's law). *1ˢᵗ Timothy 2:13, 14 (KJV)*

"Wherefore God also gave them up to uncleanness through the lusts of their own hearts, to dishonor their own bodies between themselves:

Who changed the truth of God into a lie, and worshipped and served the creature more than the creator, who is blessed forever. Amen

For this cause God gave them up unto vile affections: **for even their women did change the natural use into that which is against nature:" Romans 1:24-26 (KJV)**

Again:

"For it is a shame even to speak of those things which are done of them in secret." Ephesians 5:12 (KJV)

This kind of lifestyle should at least remain behind closed doors, and secret if practiced at all because of the shame that should be with it. Today the people are bold, and have forgotten the wrath of God on Sodom and Gomorrah, and the cities in the plains, which had pleasure in them that do them. This is not new: This will happen again according to: Romans 1:32 (KJV)

Now the males

"And likewise also the men, leaving the natural use of the woman, burned in their lust one toward another; men with men working that which is unseemly, and receiving in themselves that recompense of their error which was meet." Romans 1:24-27(KJV)

No doubt Old Testament sin and scripture revived

"Thou shall not lie with mankind, as with womankind: it is abomination. (Filthy, unclean, against nature." Leviticus 18:22 (KJV)

The book being emphatic in its words. We see that there is no room to say that God is not talking about the act of homosexuality, (not the people, for the people are: male or female and not homosexuals).

Do they have a malicious spirit against others? You judge.

"And even as they did not like to retain God in their knowledge, God gave them over to a reprobate mind, to do those things which are not convenient.

Being filled with all unrighteousness, fornication, wickedness, covetousness, maliciousness, full of envy, murder, debate, deceit, malignity; whisperers,

Backbiters, haters of God, despiteful, proud, boasters, inventors of evil things, disobedient to parents,

Without understanding, covenantbreakers, without natural affection, implacable, unmerciful:

Who knowing the judgment of God, that they which commit such things are worthy of death, not only do the same, but have pleasure in them that do them." Romans 1:28-32 (KJV)

Sexual War in this generation

When the scripture said that He turned them over to the things which we see of them; it could be construed or misconstrued as to say: let them alone, or leave them to God, but we, as a society must struggle against what the scriptures call evil, that we might save some; even our own children, which also get caught–up in the works of the devil, which means that the parents and the pastors must involve themselves in this warfare.

The church must need to be taught what thus saith the Lord concerning sexual relations, they must be taught what is legal in the law of God concerning sexual relations between couples.

"For it is not a vain thing for you; because it is your life: and through this thing ye shall prolong your days..." Deuteronomy 32:47 (KJV)

Do animals participate in such practices?

Why does a man or woman do that which an animal wouldn't do by nature? Dogs don't naturally do such things nor, rabbits, birds, worms, snakes, cats, or any such like. Every creature has their pleasures in having sex through an orgasm while reproducing themselves: or simply answering the call of the natural passion for sex which was given to every creature by God. Are animals wiser to remain with the natural use of nature more than the man? Shame on the appetite of man! But we as Christians must commit, and cling to our salvation according to the scriptures, for this is our life as we have seen in the scriptures, **but, does man believe the scriptures?**

Recompense reserved for sinners

This punishment is reserved for non-repentant sinners in the end along with Satan, and his angels. Beware!

Things revealed

Satan while in the garden approached not the man for immoral change, because the man was not his target, the woman was his target for immoral change and destruction as the weaker vessel for a lack of knowledge: (his question to the woman was; did God say?) causing the woman to contend or debate with Satan over what God said or didn't say: her not having all of the information which God had given to her husband Adam, this caused her to be deficient in knowledge when dealing with her enemy.

"Now the serpent was more subtil than any beast of the field which the LORD God had made. And he said unto the woman, yea, hath God said, ye shall not eat of every tree of the garden?" Genesis 3:1 (KJV)

Sexual war in this generation

Satan was not after the destruction of the son of God, as much as he was after the woman (the bride of Christ the church). If Satan could destroy the bride of Christ this would automatically destroy the sons and His bride, the church: the woman having no children creating no life as the church: yet.

As we know the woman in typology represents the church just as the man represents the Father:

Satan was not after the destruction of the man as son: but the woman as the bride (church) while she was in her infancy, she had birthed no children because she was yet a babe herself and yet without knowledge as to who she was or who she was purposed to become. Satan's mission was to abort her purpose as God's bride while she was yet in the garden, young and unlearned; while she was yet a babe knowing nothing, so that she, as the church, would never give birth to children as sons and daughters of Christ's body, causing her to miss her opportunity to become His bride; a glorious church.

Satan's subtility toward the woman was for information: did she know what God actually said to her husband Adam and why? Causing the woman to respond as she understood the command; which was not to partake of the tree in the midst of the garden, Satan knowing his motives was towards Christ and His future bride the Church:

Remember, he attacked Eve in the garden to change God's law with his subtility, not the man, he used this same spirit on Sarai in the same manner to set the illegitimate son of Hagar before Isaac the promised seed, when she offered Abraham her hand maiden to conceive, he used Job's wife to entice her husband to curse his God and die, him already being a son. He used the woman to change the natural use of the body to that which was against nature. Romans chapter 1.

Open your eyes people

Did you notice that he, Satan that is, never approached not one of these men at any time; not for any reason? They simply were of no interest to him, only the woman. Again, Chapter 1:26 (KJV) of Romans brings the woman to the forefront as the weaker vessel for immoral change by changing God's law concerning the natural use of the body.

Satan didn't have to do anything to destroy the man, but he had to deceive the woman into corruption with his subtility before she understood her role in the future, and before she understood that she was an instrument to be used by Christ as the church.

All of this evil was perpetrated against Christ church by Satan through the woman before she was grown, this was to destroy the church before she could carry out her assignment in this life, and glorify her God.

So sin entered into the world through Adam, but God had a remedy of salvation for us and a permanent destruction for Satan.

"And I will put enmity between thee and the woman, and between thy seed and her seed; (meaning Christ) it shall bruise thy head, and thou shall bruise his heel." Genesis 3:15 (KJV)

This is my commentary on Satan's war against the church

The premise of this point in this documentary is to expose the warfare of Satan's revenge against the Christ through the woman as the church: and God's salvation for the redemption of the woman: the sanctification, and the purifying and cleansing of her as His body (Church). Satan understood that Eve was a babe without knowledge of her position in this world, and that she would be the mother of all Humans, and as the future bride (church) she was a perfect target against Christ in his war against the church. Satan being angry because of the loss of his position in heaven sought to finish the war in the garden in the defeat of God through the woman, His church. Man is now positioned in God's heart; again, being perfected as he once was through the man's faith in the resurrected Christ, our Lord and saviour Jesus Christ.

Man is being saved from eternal damnation, being justified freely by His grace, and being justified by His blood.

"Being justified freely by His grace, through the redemption that is in Christ Jesus." Romans 3:34 (KJV)

"Much more then, being now justified by His blood, we shall be saved from wrath through Him." Romans 5:9 (KJV)

…Knowing this, that our old man is crucified with Him, that the body of sin might be destroyed, that henceforth we should not serve sin. Romans 6:4-6 (KJV)

So Satan took advantage of the woman while she was in her youth to cause her to be defiled, spoiled and unclean in her infancy, even though she would live; she would live forever in an ungodly state: having breath but not eternal life being aborted. And if she would partake of the tree of life in her ungodly state: she would die in her sin with no hope of redemption. This was Satan's plan for God's creation, even today his plan is that we would die in our sins, with no hope of eternal life.

Had Satan succeeded in permanently defiling the woman as the bride of Christ, with no escape through the blood of Jesus: Satan would have won his war over God which he started in heaven when he decided to take it over, and was kicked out. He sought to finish his war on the earth in the garden, but, again, he is defeated by the LORD God Jesus Christ. Hallelujah! Satan, as hard as he tried: could not destroy the structure of the Church.

Lucifer's attitude toward God

"How art thou fallen from heaven, O Lucifer, Son of the morning! How art thou cut down to the ground, which didst weaken the nations! For thou hath said in thine heart, I will ascend into heaven, I will exalt my throne above the stars of God: I will sit also upon the mount of the congregation, in the sides of the North

I will ascend above the heights of the clouds; I will be like the most high. Yet thou shalt be brought down to hell, to the sides of the pit." Isaiah 14:12-15 (KJV)

But inspite of all these set-backs: the battle worn woman, the church: wins! Maybe the woman is not the weaker vessel after all, maybe it is Lucifer himself, the one which has created so much havoc with the woman as the church. He fell into his own snare because of jealousy and his own deceit, deceiving his own heart. Be not deceived!

Revelation said

"He that overcometh shall inherit all things; and I will be his God, and he shall be my son. But the fearful, and unbelieving, and the abominable, and murderers, and whoremongers, and sorcerers, and idolaters, and all liars, shall have their part in the lake which burneth with fire and brimstone: which is the second death." Revelation 21:7, 8 (KJV)

There is a price to be paid

"For who hath known the mind of the Lord, that he may instruct Him? But we have the mind of Christ." 1st Corinthians 2:16 (KJV)

"Who hath directed the Spirit of the LORD, or being His counsellor hath taught Him? With whom took He counsel, and who instructed Him, and taught Him in the path of judgment, and taught Him knowledge, and shewed Him the way of understanding?" Isaiah 40:13,14 (KJV)

"Seeing it is a righteous thing with God to recompense (meaning to repay) tribulation to them that trouble you; And to you who are troubled rest with us, when the Lord Jesus shall be revealed from heaven with His mighty angels, In flaming fire taking vengeance on them that know not God, and that obey not the gospel of our Lord Jesus Christ: Who shall be punished with everlasting destruction from the presence of the Lord, and from the glory of His power; When He shall come to be glorified in His saints, and to be admired in all them that believe (because our testimony among you was believed) in that day." 2nd Thessalonians 1:6-10 (KJV)

Questions from the Author:

Will this book cause you to do a daily self evaluation? If so, how?

Reflection:

_____

_____

_____

_____

_____

_____

_____

_____

_____

_____

_____

_____

_____

_____

_____

_____

_____

_____

_____

_____

CHAPTER VI

Does Jesus discriminate? NO! The question is a sin question.

First let me express my thoughts on the question, does Jesus discriminate?

This means that we first must determine if Jesus, the judge, is evil? NO! He, Jesus that is, is no respecter of person, according to Romans 2:11 (KJV) which *saith, **for there is no respect of persons with God**.

The next question would be, Is Jesus righteous? Yes! So all judgment by Him must be right according to. Romans 2:2. (KJV) which saith:

"But we are sure that the judgment of God is according to truth against them which commit such things.

God concluding all under sin which saith, but the scriptures hath concluded all under sin, that the promise by faith of Jesus Christ might be given to them that believe." According to Galatians 3:22 (KJV)

"Which saith, all have sinned and come short of the glory of God Romans." 3:23 (KJV)

So the punishment of hell for sinners applies to all classes, gender, race, creed, nationality, sexual orientation and color of people; which commit such and die in their unrepented sin. This is the penalty or price we must pay for the pleasures of sin, if we choose not to repent, and turn to God and from sin. According to the scriptures.

"But the fearful, and unbelieving, and the abominable, and murderers, and whoremongers, and sorcerers, and Idolaters, and all liars, shall have their part in the lake which burneth with fire and brimstone: which is the second death." According to Revelation 21:8 (KJV)

This group of sinners is described, and is reminded of the penalty for their unrepented sins.

"Know ye not that the unrighteous shall not inherit the kingdom of God? Be not deceived: neither fornicators, nor Idolaters, nor adulterers, nor effeminate, nor abusers of themselves with mankind, nor thieves, nor covetous, nor drunkards, nor revilers, nor extortioners, shall inherit the kingdom of God." 1st Corinthians 6:9-11 (KJV)

This salvation happened to us because, we were called to salvation, we heard the word, and the voice of God, and believed the word which we heard, repented of our sins and were baptized, or washed in His name for the remission of our sin which we had committed, applying the blood, the cleansing agent to our sins.

Now we are clean and justified in His sight, through His blood. Salvation is in Jesus Christ alone: thru His blood. (Sacrifice)

No law, no judgement

"For until the law sin was in the world: but sin is not imputed when there is no law." Romans 5:13(KJV)

"Because the law worketh wrath: for where no law is, there is no transgression;" Romans 4:15 (KJV).

But now there is the law of God to all that work righteousness. Romans 2, again.

"But we are sure that the judgment of God is according to truth against them which commit such things. And thinkest thou this, O man, that judges them which do such things, and dost the same, that thou shall escape the judgment of God? Or despises thou the riches of His goodness and forbearance and longsuffering; not knowing that the goodness of God leadeth thee to repentance?

But after thy hardness and impenitent heart treasurest up unto thyself wrath against the day of wrath and revelation of the righteous judgment of God: Who will render to every man according to his deeds. To them by patience continuance in well doing seek for glory and honour and immortality, eternal life:

But unto them that are contentious, and do not obey the truth, but obey unrighteousness, indignation and wrath, Tribulation and anguish, upon every soul of man that doeth evil, **of the Jew first,** *and* **also of the gentile***; But glory, honour, and peace, to every man that* **worketh good, to the Jew first,** *and* **also to the gentile: For there is no respect of persons with God." Romans 2:2-11 (KJV)**

These are the final points to the LGBT community and the general populace: concerning God's view on gender difference, and His punishment to all that disagree with His process and judgment for the human lifestyles.

The Christian lifestyle.

When the babes are born into the church, he or she must become aware of what is good for him or her as social behaviors. Our lifestyle must completely change. The clubs and the commonplaces we once frequented which was pleasurable to us, Smoking, drinking alcohol, cussing, doing drugs, having illegal sexual affairs, solicitations, and all such must no longer be a part of our social lifestyle.

For now we are clean, through the spirit and the word, by the washing of water. We are commanded by the scriptures as Christians to live a holy lifestyle. St. John 15:3 (KJV)

Now ye are clean through the word which I have spoken unto you.

"Having therefore these promises, dearly beloved, let us cleanse ourselves from all filthiness of the flesh and spirit, perfecting holiness in the fear of God." 2nd Corinthians 7:1(KJV)

"What? Know ye not that your body is the temple of the Holy Ghost which is in you, which ye have of God, and you are not your own? For ye are bought with a price: therefore glorify God in your body, and in your spirit, which are God's." 1st Corinthian 6:19, 20. (KJV)

"I beseech you therefore, brethren, by the mercies of God, that you present your bodies a living sacrifice, holy, acceptable unto God, which is your reasonable service." Romans 12:1. (KJV)

"Abstain from all appearance of evil. And the very God of peace, sanctify you wholly; and I pray God your whole spirit and soul and body be preserved blameless unto the coming of the Lord Jesus Christ" 1st Thessalonians 5:22, 23. (KJV)

"Forasmuch then as Christ hath suffered for us in the flesh, arm yourselves likewise with the same mind: for he that hath suffered in the flesh hath ceased from sin; that he no longer should live the rest of his time in the flesh to the lust of men, but to the will of God. For the time past of our life may suffice us to have wrought the will of the Gentiles, when we walked in lasciviousness, lust, excess of wine, revellings, banqueting, and abominable idolatries.

Wherein they think it strange that ye run not with them to the same excess of riot, speaking evil of you who shall give account to Him that is ready to judge the quick and the dead. For this cause was the gospel preached also to them that are dead, that they might be judged according to men in the flesh, but live according to God in the spirit." 1ˢᵗ Peter 4:1-6. (KJV

"If you then be risen with Christ, seek those things which are above, where Christ sitteth on the right hand of God. Set your affections on things above, not on things on the earth. For ye are dead, and your life is hid with Christ in God. When Christ, who is our life, shall appear, then shall ye also appear with Him in glory?

Modified therefore your members which are upon the earth; fornication, uncleanness, inordinate affection, evil concupiscence, and covetousness, which is idolatry: For which things sake, the wrath of God cometh on the children of disobedience. In the which ye also walk some time, when you lived in them.

But now ye also put off all these; anger: wrath: malice, blasphemy: filthy communications out of your mouth. Lie not one to another, seeing that you have put off the old man with his deeds; and have put on the new man, which is renewed in knowledge after the image of Him that created him." Colossians 3:1-10. (KJV)

These are the negative things that newborn babies must no longer be involved with anymore, which were their previous lifestyle.

What are the positive things that a newborn saint must do?

"Put on therefore, as the elect of God, holy and beloved, bowels of mercies, kindness, humbleness of mind, meekness, long-suffering; Forbearing one another, and forgiving one another, if any man have a quarrel against any: even as Christ forgave you, so also, do ye.

And above all these things put on charity, which is the bond of perfectness. And let the peace of God rule in your hearts, to the which also ye are called in one body; and be ye thankful." Colossians 3:14, 15. (KJV)

When we begin to live this type of lifestyle, through the preaching and teaching of the pastor, (scriptures) then we are moving into God's perfection as New Testament saints. This is speaking of this new growth in Christ, as a light to the world, and we must practice this word of God. How long you ask?

'Till we all come into the unity of the faith, and the knowledge of the son of God, unto a perfect man, unto the measure of the stature of the fulness of Christ:

That we henceforth be no more children, tossed to and fro and carried about with every wind of doctrine, by the slight of men, and cunning craftiness, whereby lie in wait to deceive;

But speaking the truth in love, may grow up into Him in all things, which is the head, even Christ:

For the whole body fitly joined together and compacted by that which every joint supplieth, according to the effectual working in the measure of every part, maketh increase of the body unto the edifying of itself in love." Ephesians 4:12-16 (KJV)

So the need for the Pastors, Prophets, Evangelist and Teachers are for the perfecting of the saints verse 11.

The Apostles are forever with us, because the biblical words which we read and hear are the Apostles, and not a living speaking entity on earth, but the word already spoken, which we as saints must follow; this is the straight and narrow way.

The Pastor is the overseer or Bishop of the flock.

Pastors are to take heed to themselves to represent God well, he must be blameless: full of the Holy Ghost, wisdom, knowledge and the word.

A. He must give account to God for every soul who comes into the local church under his pastoral ship.

B. He is the watchmen who ministers to the spiritual welfare of the membership.

C. The directions are given to the membership for stability of each member.

D. Do not hesitate to ask the Pastor for his assistance in anything.

"Take heed therefore unto yourselves, and to all the flock, over the which the Holy Ghost hath made you overseers, to feed the church of God, which He hath purchased with His own blood." Acts 20:28 &32(KJV)

"And now brethren, I commend you to God, and to the word of His grace, which is able to build you up, and to give you an inheritance among all them which are sanctified." Acts 14:23 (KJV)

If the pastor can't help you, then he should connect you with the proper agency that should be able to assist you, even in the membership.

We have determined that the Fellowship inside the church should be more free and safe than any other place, it is supposed to be a place of strength and fellowship. According to:

"Now the Lord is that spirit: and where the spirit of the Lord is, there is liberty." 2nd Corinthians 3:17 (KJV)

We know how we expect the church to be spotless and perfect, but it is in most cases just the opposite, because the world has come into the church through the people which are coming out of the world into the church, and while they are coming straight from out of the world; they are bringing all of their worldly lifestyle with them.

This means that the church assembly is not spotless, and sometimes the older Saints are a little cranky, but that's part of life and our growth in learning how to deal with the Saints, and the worldly newcomers.

As new born babies they should try their best to get involved in a regular Bible teaching course at their local church.

I know most people have a little trepidation when they come into the church about positions and what they're capable of doing. Their questions may be: do they have talent, what is their ministry, who's available to help them, and whether they will be a failure.

These are questions that will be coming before them, because the enemy doesn't want them; the new convert to get involved in anything spiritual. Satan's goal is to keep the Christians weak and vulnerable to his wiles.

Authority in the church

"All scripture is given by inspiration of God, and is profitable for doctrine, for reproof, for correction, for instruction in righteousness." 2nd Timothy 3:16 (KJV)

"Preach the word, be instant in season, out of season; reprove, rebuke, exhort with all longsuffering and doctrine." 2nd Timothy 4:2 (KJV)

"Them that sin rebuke before all, that others may also fear." 1st Timothy 5:20(KJV)

"Obey them that have the rule over you, and submit yourselves: for they watch for your souls, as they must give account, that they may do it with joy, and not with grief: for that is unprofitable for you." Hebrews 13:17 (KJV))

Questions from the Author:

How do you rate yourself as a modern day sanctified woman, or otherwise, using a scale of 0-10.

Reflection:

_____

_____

_____

_____

_____

_____

_____

_____

_____

_____

_____

_____

_____

_____

_____

_____

_____

_____

_____

_____

CHAPTER VII

An Introduction to love. Does love work?

We previously spoke a little about the mind of God, prophecy, the Garden experience of Adam and Eve, and how the law blessed us. We said all scriptures led to Christ and His redemptive process and we spoke about how Jesus will counter effect the actions of Adam.

We looked at how to find salvation, baptism of the Holy Ghost, maintaining good works, and coming forth. We also spoke about the road to salvation. Then we came down to lessons taught, questions were asked, we spoke about laying on of the hands, then we spoke on the things new converts must put away; sins of the flesh.

Then we saw the fruit of the spirit and its effects in Christian living, after that we got into the ordinance of the church, and how not to offend others. Then we asked the question, is there a triune God. Then we spoke about dress and attire. After that, we spoke about the LGBT community in the church, with no negativity here. The Christian lifestyle, pastoral oversight and we're not done, and we will be going back to speak about the baptism and see a few other things as we've grown in the church.

New subject.

Let us attempt to speak on love. We've seen the sins of the flesh, and we said that these are the things that we must let go of, seeing, we are not to be partakers of them any longer being Christians.

We found that people that do such things shall not inherit the kingdom of God. And our goal is to live with God presently and in the end. 1st Corinthians 6:9 (KJV)

These are the no, no's in life

"Envyings, murders, drunkenness, revellings, and such like: of the which I tell you before, as I have told you in time past, that they which do such things shall not inherit the kingdom of God." Galatians 5:21 (KJV)

The subject of love deals with the positive side of holiness, it has to do with our Christian walk as the results of our salvation, and being filled with the Holy Ghost.

An introduction to Love, Does Love Work

You might ask the question, does the Holy Ghost have that much affect in our lives?

This is the Practical Side of Salvation

The love walk, or the Christian walk is the greatest part of salvation, after we have been endued with the power of the Holy Ghost. Without the power of the Holy Ghost we cannot endure heartache, nor overcome temptation. This is the utter most purpose of the plan of salvation, that is, for us to live in Christ, and for Christ to live in us: to destroy the works of the devil, and this also is to cause all to love one another.

This is not a religious myth but a sincere demonstration of kindness one towards another.

The total message of Jesus Christ was to teach us how to love one another, and to destroy the works of the devil, and to save us from sin:"

"A new commandment I give unto you, that ye love one another; as I have loved you, that ye also love one another.

By this shall all men know that you are my disciples, if you have love one to another." St. John 13:34, 35 (KJV)

This is the same love that Jesus demonstrated to us in: St. John 3:16. (KJV) This one love is where Jesus gave all: withholding nothing, and this is the requirement that He requires of us withholding nothing from each other in love.

The walk of the Christian would be in the fruit of the spirit. When we can identify the fruit; then we understand what is meant by the fruit of the spirit. The fruit of the Spirit is the attributes of unconditional love, because this is one fruit paired into sections. And these paired sections of the fruit are found in: Galatian 5:22-25 (KJV)

And they are: *"Love, joy, peace, long-suffering, gentleness, goodness, faith,*

Meekness, temperance: against such there is no law.

And they that are Christ have crucified the flesh with the affections and lust.

If we live in the Spirit, let us also walk in the spirit.

The Spirit brings into our lives great principles. This is a thought I haven't thought much about on my own, but it's worth looking into; new saints, and old saints should do the same.

Love: this is the love that loves all. The one love, the universal care for all.

"For God so loved the world that He gave his only begotten son, that whosoever believes in Him should not perish." St. John 3:16. (KJV)

This is an unselfish love. The divine love of God. What can compare to this love: but this is what we must practice to do daily.

Phileo: this is the love that fails, the love that can change into hate, this is not God's love, and there is a great difference between God's love and other loves.

The romance love, and a mother's love, and the love of a friend are conditional, but Gods' love is permanent, undying even when it brings us sadness.

The attributes of love

Let us talk about this true love for a moment; love is like music, it moves your soul or your being, whether or not you want to be moved by it. Music penetrates the spirit so does love much more than music: that's why love is such a wonderful and powerful tool. Love silently penetrates a hardened heart and causes it to become softened and become tenderer. Love is what Jesus used as His offering to the Father, as we are to do in representing Him.

God's love never increases nor does it diminish, because of its perfection from the beginning, so there is no room for growth or decline in His love. All other types of love do eventually fail.

The prophet was told by God to go to Zarephath, God said that He had commanded a widow woman there to sustain him, in this time of famine.

"So he arose and went to Zarephath. And when he came to the gate of the city, behold, the widow woman was

gathering of sticks: and he called to her, and said, fetch me I pray thee, a little water in a vessel, that I may drink. And as she was going to fetch it, he called to her, and said, bring me, I pray thee, a morsel of bread in thine hand. And she said, as the LORD thy God liveth, I have not a cake, but an handful of meal in a barrel, and a little oil in a cruse: and behold, I am gathering two sticks, that I may go in and dress it for me and my son, that we may eat it, and die.

And Elijah said unto her, fear not; go and do as thou hast said: but make me thereof a little cake first, and bring it unto me, and after make for thee and thy son. For thus saith the LORD God of Israel, Thy barrel of meal shall not waste, neither shall the cruse of oil fail, until the day that the Lord sendeth rain upon the earth.

And she went and did according to the saying of Elijah: and she, and he, and her house, did eat many days. And the barrel of meal wasted not, neither did the cruse of oil fail, according to the word of the LORD, which He spake by Elijah." 1ˢᵗ *Kings 17: 10-15 (KJV)*

This woman gave all out of love and obedience to her God, not as much as to the prophet, as we remember: **God commanded her to sustain the prophet out of her nothing, He, requiring all from her. These are our examples, always search the scriptures for your answers to any situation, even though you may not like nor except the answer.**

Out of God's love for His creation, He gave all: even though we were not His children as yet. What? Yes, not yet His children, because we had not received the new (spiritual birth yet) but He gave all that He possessed inspite of that. He loved those which loved Him not.

"... Now if any man have not the spirit of Christ he is none of His. Romans 8:9 (KJV)

But I say unto you which hear, Love your enemies, and do good to them which hate you.

Bless them that curse you, and pray for them which spitefully use you.

For if you love them which love you, what thanks have ye? For sinners also love those that love them.

But love your enemies, and do good, and lend, hoping for nothing again; and your reward shall be great, and ye shall be the children of the highest: for He is kind to the unthankful and the evil.

Be ye therefore merciful, as your Father also is merciful. Why call ye me, Lord, Lord, and do not what I say?" Luke 6:27-49; 27, 28; 32, 35, 36; 46 (KJV)

I have concluded that God's Love does work, and will always work and sustain us.

Introduction to Love, Does Love Work?

A Sanctified Church

All people must be taught the doctrine of God according to the apostle's teachings, that is, that which is written: that they may be able to become a part of His body living in Christ. John 17:20-b (KJV)

"Whosoever transgresseth, and abideth not in the doctrine of Christ, has not God. He that abideth in the doctrine of Christ, he has both the Father and the son. If there come any unto you, and bring not this doctrine, receive him not into your house, neither bid him God speed: For he that biddeth him God speed is partaker of his evil deeds." 2ⁿᵈ John 9-11 (KJV)

Even though there have been a falling away from the faith, Jesus has many more hungry and thirsty souls coming into His body out of love and recognition of who He is. Some are receiving Christ again, for the first true time: by the learned doctrine of the apostles, and some of them are coming for the first time to be saved. Thank God!

"Now the spirit speaketh expressly, that in the latter times some shall depart from the faith, giving heed to seducing spirits, and doctrines of devils," 1ˢᵗ Timothy 4:1 (KJV)

God can't use anyone that's not teaching His doctrine for a lack of faith, for without faith, you cannot please God. The Scripture saith.

"But without faith it is impossible to please Him: for he that cometh to God must believe that He is, and that He is a rewarder of them that diligently seek Him." Hebrews 11:6 (KJV)

"But, though we, or an angel from heaven, preach any other gospel unto you than that which we have preached unto you, let him be accursed." Galatian 1:8. (KJV)

"If any man teach otherwise, and consent not to wholesome words, even the words of our Lord Jesus Christ, and to the doctrine, which is according to godliness; Perverse disputings of men of corrupt minds, and destitute of the truth, supposing that gain is godliness: From such withdraw yourself" 1ˢᵗ Timothy 6:3, 5. (KJV)

"'Now we command you, brethren, in the name of our Lord Jesus Christ that ye withdraw yourselves from every brother that walketh disorderly, and not after the tradition in which he received of us." 2ⁿᵈ Thessalonian 3:6 (KJV)

"Now I beseech you, brethren, mark them which caused division and offenses. Contrary to the doctrine which you have learned; and avoid them:" Romans 16:17. (KJV)

"But now I have written unto you, not to keep company, if any man that is called a Brother, be a fornicator, or

covetousness, or an idolater, or a railer, or a drunkard, or an extortion, with such and one no not to eat." 1ˢᵗ Corinthians 5:11 (KJV)

"A man that is a heretic after the first and second ammunition reject; Knowing that he that is such is subverted, and being condemned of himself." Titus 3:10, 11. (KJV)

"Peter said," but there were false prophets also among the people, even as there shall be false teachers among you, who privately shall bring in damnable heresies, even denying the Lord that brought them, and bring upon themselves swift destruction."
2ⁿᵈ Peter 2:1 (KJV)

So the church must be holy unto God and set apart from the world and sin.

Questions from the Author:

Do you have a need or desire for forgiveness from God or others, if so, how would you begin the process?

Reflection:

_____

_____

_____

_____

_____

_____

_____

_____

_____

_____

_____

_____

_____

_____

_____

_____

_____

_____

_____

_____

CHAPTER VIII

Introduction to Love, Eternal Security

Seeing there is a great controversy concerning eternal security, a new convert more than any other must hear what the word of God has to say concerning the scriptures that doomed us to hell. It is imperative to know the truth concerning our salvation: Whether or not we are saved while sinning.

Question: Is it true that a person is eternally secured or saved: once he or she has experienced salvation: whether he lives a constant holy life or not?

Constantly the scriptures tell us that there are conditions to this salvation; whether we accept that fact or not, beginning with the following words. Verse 23 of Colossians said, **if we continue.**

"For it pleased the Father that In Him should all fulness dwell; And, having made peace through the blood of His cross, by Him to reconcile all things unto Himself; by Him, I say, whether they be things in earth, or things in heaven. And you, that were sometime alienated and enemies in your mind by wicked works, yet now hath He reconciled

In the body of His flesh through death, to present you holy and unblameable and unreproveable in His sight:

If we continue in the faith grounded and settled, and be not moved away from the hope of the gospel, which ye have heard, and which was preached to every creature which is under heaven; whereof I Paul am made a minister;" Colossians 1:19-23

"Let that therefore abide in you, which ye have heard from the beginning, if that which ye have heard from the beginning shall remain in you, ye also shall continue in the son, and in the Father.

And this is the promise that He hath promised us, even eternal life.

These things have I written unto you concerning them that seduce you." 1ˢᵗ John 2:24-25 (KJV)

Some say that we are eternally saved, because Jesus took it all to the cross for us, He is then placed into the hands of God, where no man or power can pluck him out. This is one of the scriptures that seems to fit their doctrine. But does it?

Jesus said: *"Verily, verily, I say unto you, he that believes on me has everlasting life." St John 6:47 (KJV)*

They use this sort of scripture to support the doctrine; once saved always saved.

However, *"the wages of sin is still death." Romans 6:23 (KJV)*

My school of thought on this scripture.

Number one: in St. John's Gospel Jesus was not teaching the New Testament church this message, this message went to the Jews in a different dispensation. Also, Jesus was trying to convince the nonbelieving Jews to believe, and except Him as their Lord and Christ: So Jesus could bring belief to them, that, which is faith; then the explanation of it would have been given. Let's move on.

Now the question remains, in this day, is it once saved always saved? The Scriptures which talk about escape, calling it the pollution of the world, and grace, and to keep yourself clean, and in the love of God, leave us no room for sinning willingly, according to the scripture. Again;

"For If after they have escaped the pollution of the world through the knowledge of the Lord and Savior Jesus Christ, they are again entangled therein, and overcome, the latter end is worse with them than the beginning."

"For it had been better for them not to have known the way of righteousness, than, after they have known it, to turn from the holy commandment delivered unto them." 2nd Peter 2:20, 21 (KJV)

Here Matthew is showing us that we are worse sinning that second time, than we were when we were sinning the first time.

"When the unclean spirit is gone out of a man, he walketh through dry places, seeking rest, and findeth none. Then he saith, I will return into my house from whence I came out; and when he is come, he findeth it empty, swept, and garnished."

"Then goeth he, and taketh with himself, seven other spirits more wicked than himself, and they enter in and dwell there: and the last state of that man is worse than the first. Even so shall it be also unto this wicked generation." Matthew 12:43- 45. (KJV)

More warnings from the Scripture on the subject.

"Looking diligently least any man failed of the grace of God: lest any root of bitterness springing up trouble you, and thereby many be defiled;

Least there be any fornicator, or profane person, as Esau, who for one morsel of meat sold his birthright.

For ye know how that afterwards, when he would have inherited the blessing, he was rejected: for he found no place of repentance, though he sought it carefully with tears." Hebrews 12:15-17. (KJV)

If we study the Bible at all; or casually read it, we come across Scripture that help us to understand right from wrong, the facts from the myths, and it puts a stop to our opinions. Then it's up to us to choose life, putting forth our hand to the tree of the knowledge of good and evil, or the tree of life. Again, for the second time; to choose life or death.

The Scriptures continually offer us that choice. *"As He said, I have set before you an open door." Revelation 3:8. (KJV)*

So our way of escape is to measure our own growth continually in Christ by his word. 2nd Peter 1. Gives us a simple measuring chart:

"And besides this, giving all diligence, add to your faith virtue; and to virtue knowledge;

And to knowledge temperance; and to temperance patience; and to patience godliness;

And to godliness brotherly kindness; and to brotherly kindness charity.

For if these things be in you, and abound, they make you that ye shall neither be barren nor unfruitful in the knowledge of our Lord Jesus Christ.

But he that lacking these things is blind, and cannot see, afar, and has forgotten that he was purged from his old sins.

Wherefore the rather, brethren, give diligence to make your calling and election sure: but if we do these things, you shall never fall." 2nd Peter 1:5-10 (KJV)

Here we see God gives us a place and a way, and the acknowledgement to know how to escape, how not to fall, but how to remain steadfast, unmovable, always abounding in **the love of God.**

"Keep yourselves in the love of God, for the mercy of our Lord Jesus Christ unto eternal life.

Now unto Him that is able to keep you from falling, and to present you faultless before the presence of His glory with exceed in joy." Jude 21, 24. (KJV)

Note this

This is the love of God toward man, for we are Saved by Grace, and Kept by His Grace.

"For the grace of God that brings salvation has appeared to all men,

Teaching us that, denying ungodliness and worldly lusts, we should live soberly, righteously, and godly, in this present world; Who gave Himself for us that He might redeem us from all iniquity, and purify unto Himself a peculiar people, zealous of good works." Titus 2:11- 12, 14. (KJV)

"That being justified by His grace, we should be made heirs according to the hope of eternal life.

This is a faithful saying, and these things I will that thou affirm constantly, that they which have believed in God might be careful to maintain good works. These things are good and profitable unto men." Titus 3:7, 8. (KJV)

"For I know thy works: behold, I have set before thee an open door, and no man can shut it:" Revelation 3:8 (KJV)

From these Scriptures, we find that grace saves us from our past sins, so that we might walk in newness of life, in this present world.

"Whom God hath set forth to be a propitiation through faith in His blood, to declare His righteousness for the remission of sins that are past, through the forbearance of God:

To declare, I say, at this time His righteousness: that He might be just, and the justifier of which believeth in Jesus." Romans 3:25-26 (KJV)

"By grace are ye saved through faith; and that not of yourselves: it is the gift of God:

Not of works, least any man should boast." Ephesians 2:8-9 (KJV)

Introduction to Love, Eternal Security

Question, how does good works play into our salvation process?

We must know for a surety that this is the work of God: that no man can glory in this, but it's not the work of Grace alone, that we must also maintain good works through Him. Good works does not merit our salvation;

"As it is written, there is none that is righteous, no, not one:

There is none that understandeth, there is none that seeketh after God.

Therefore by the deeds of the law, there shall no flesh be justified in His sight: for by the law is the knowledge of sin." *Romans 3:10, 11, 20. (KJV)*

The scriptures explanation

In order for God to save us, He concluded all to be classified as unholy and not worthy of salvation. God did not save us by mere grace alone. Though grace is used as a means of justification. According to the scripture. The scripture hath concluded all under sin that the promise by faith of Jesus Christ might be given to them that believe. Galatians 3:22 (KJV)

"Which saith, for all have sinned, and come short of the glory of God;" *Romans 3: 23, (KJV)*

"It was not done by grace only, for by grace are ye saved through faith; and that not of yourselves:" *Ephesians 2: 8 (KJV)*

It was not done by grace only. Justification is also meted out to us through or by faith.

"What shall we say then that Abraham our father, as pertaining to the flesh, has found?
For if Abraham were justified by works, he hath whereof to glory; but not before God."
Romans 4:1-2 (KJV)

This means that we must put our trust in the one Jesus Christ, (not Abraham nor any other) who is accredited as keeping the law, and was declared by God to be righteous.

And therefore the propitiation and the gift of His righteousness for our sins were to be forgiven to everyone who believes in Jesus Christ. This we received.

No 1. Belief – by our faith. 2. Grace – justifies the work of Christ. 3. Faith – by grace. 4. Christ at Calvary. - We all have sinned. 5. Washing – baptizing in His blood. We listed: belief, grace, faith, Calvary, and His blood.

Now we will speak more fully about each.

For the Scripture saith:

"Much more then, being now justified by His blood, we shall be saved from wrath through Him." Romans 5:9. (KJV)

We have heard from the beginning that; the shedding of the blood was the only thing that removes sin.

We often say that salvation is free, however, someone had to pay the price for our sins, and in paying: something or someone had to die by the shedding of the blood.

Salvation is free to us, because we didn't have to pay the sin price in death like Jesus did, but the work of salvation is by grace, through faith and in completing the steps of salvation.

So then, these three means of justification, by grace, by faith, and by His blood has to be exercised to obtain the forgiveness of sin, so that God may save all from their sins.

Now Satan hath no more power over death concerning us. Our lives and our salvation is up to us, as to whether we choose life thru the word of God, or whether we choose death thru the tradition of men, and the spirit of Satan. So don't give your power of freedom back to Satan, which Christ has bought back for you with His own blood. (Sacrifice)

Introduction to Love, Jesus took his Power

When Satan over-took Adam and Eve in the Garden: his plan was to destroy God's creation and the future church: aborting the future sons and daughters through death because of disobedience: for after their disobedience death did reign.

For the scriptures had said that they would surely die.

"And the Lord **God Commanded the MAN,** *saying, of every tree of the garden thou mayest freely eat:*

But of the tree of the knowledge of good and evil, thou shall not eat of it: for in the day that thou eatest thereof thou shall surely die." Genesis 2:16,17 (KJV)

Satan hath no more power over us through that eternal death: before the law was imputed Satan had power over every man through death, after he caused Adam through his wife "the so called weaker vessel" to sin, then the law came and gave man a way to escape the power of death from Satan's evil works, and to lay hold on eternal life; through the perfect redemptive process of God.

Notice the Process of Escape

The scripture said that: *"But God commendeth His love toward us, in that, while we were yet sinners, Christ died for us.*

Much more then, being now justified by His blood, we shall be saved from wrath through Him.

For if, when we were enemies, we were reconciled to God by the death of His son, much more, being reconciled, we shall be saved by His life.

And not only so, but we also joy in God through our Lord Jesus Christ, by whom we have now received the Atonement.

Wherefore, as by one man sin entered into the world, and death by sin; so death passed upon all men, for that all have sinned:"

"For until the law sin was in the world: but sin is not imputed when there is no law.

Nevertheless death reigned from Adam to Moses, even over them that had not sinned after the similitude of Adam's transgression, who is the figure of Him that is to come. Romans 5:8-21

Satan hath no more power over us through death

(Satan had the power of death over all people because of the disobedience of Adam, so all died in sin without the law of forgiveness, because without the law there were no charges brought against Cain. Even though Able's blood cried to God out of the ground for justice.) Cain escaped the charges of his Brother Abel's death, and the death penalty that was given later when the law came by Moses. At that time there was no law imputed to justify any punishment or death, so God marked Cain that no man could kill him because there was no law, or no precedent set to judge his case. So God sent him away, because there was no law of sin imputed to justify the punishment of the Law of Moses, as was later meted out as the death penalty.

"Because the law worketh wrath: for where no law is, there is no transgression. (No law was broken." Romans 4:15 (KJV)

"For until the law sin was in the world: but sin is not imputed when there is no law.

Nevertheless death reigned from Adam to Moses, even over them that had not sinned after the similitude of Adam's transgression, who is the figure of Him that was to come.

So Cain was free from punishment even though he sinned by killing his brother, Able. He broke no law.

But not as the offence, so also is the free gift. For through the offence of one many be dead, much more the grace of God. And the gift by grace, which is by one man, Jesus Christ, hath abounded unto many." Romans 5:13-15(KJV)

"And not as it was by one that sinned, so is the gift: for the judgment was by one to condemnation, but the free gift is of many offences unto justification.

For by ones man's offence death reigned by one; much more they receive abundance of grace and of the gift of righteousness shall reign in life by one, Jesus Christ.

Therefore as by the offence of one judgement came upon all men unto condemnation; even so by the righteousness of one the free gift came upon all men unto justification of life.

For as by one man's disobedience many were made sinners, so by the obedience of one shall be made righteous." Romans 5:16-19 (KJV)

"Moreover the law entered, that the offence might abound, but where sin abounded, grace did much more abound:

That as sin hath reigned unto death, even so might grace reign through righteousness unto eternal life by Jesus Christ our Lord." Romans 5:8-21 (KJV)

Shout Hallelujah!

"What shall we say then? Shall we continue in sin, that grace may abound? God forbid. How shall we, that are dead to sin, live any longer therein?

Know ye not, that so many of us as were baptized into Jesus Christ were baptized into His death? Therefore we are buried with Him by baptism into death: that like as Christ was raised up from the dead by the glory of the Father, even so we also should walk in newness of life.

For if we have been planted together in the likeness of His death, we shall also be in the likeness of His resurrection: Knowing this, that our old man is crucified with Him, that the body might be destroyed, that henceforth we should not serve sin.

For he that is dead is free from sin. Now if we be dead with Christ, we believe that we shall also live with Him: Knowing that Christ being raised from the dead dieth no more; death hath no more dominion over Him.

For in that He died; He died unto sin once: but in that He liveth, He liveth unto God. Likewise reckon ye also yourselves to be dead indeed unto sin, but alive unto God through Jesus Christ our Lord.

Let not sin therefore reign in your mortal body, that ye should obey it in the lusts thereof. Neither yields ye your members as instruments of unrighteousness unto sin: but yield yourselves unto God, as those that are alive from the dead, and your members as instruments of righteousness unto God.

"For sin shall not have dominion over you: for ye are not under the law, but under grace. What then? Shall we sin, because we are not under the law, but under grace? God forbid.

Know ye not, that to whom ye yield yourselves servants to obey, his servants ye are to whom ye obey; whether of sin unto death, or of obedience unto righteousness? But God be thanked, that ye were the servants of sin, but ye have obeyed from the heart that form of doctrine which was delivered to you.

Being then made free from sin, ye became the servants of righteousness. I speak after the manner of men because of the infirmity of your flesh: for as ye have yielded your members servants to uncleanness and to iniquity unto iniquity; even so now yield your members servants to righteousness unto holiness.

For when ye were the servants of sin, ye were free from righteousness. What fruit had ye then in those things whereof ye are now ashamed? For the end of those things is death.

But now being made free from sin, and become servants to God, ye have unto holiness, and the everlasting life. For the wages of sin is death; but the gift of God is eternal life through Jesus Christ our Lord." Romans 6:1-26 (KJV)

Since we cannot live right to be saved, and could not be excused from the death penalty, so Christ came and did all of this for us without any works on our part, except through faith, and the steps of salvation. This must be understood by sinners, new converts, and longtime Christians. That is; there was no laboring works performed by us, that is. Paying the price for sin by death. By which we were saved. This work was performed before our salvation began. Before the foundation of the world was laid; before man was created and because God had already performed the work, and set all things in place for our salvation. It does not license us to sin after our salvation and still claim eternal salvation practicing sin. If this is the case, then no man would have to live right, nor live a sanctified life, separated from the world..

These are my arguments concerning God's love, and his plan for our salvation. There is no other plan outside of this plan of salvation other than the one we've spoken on. Paul said,

"Now I beseech you, brethren, mark them which cause divisions and offenses. Contrary to the doctrine which you have learned; and avoid them." Romans 16:17 (KJV)

"As I besought thee to abide still at Ephesus, when I went into Macedonia that thou might charge some that they teach no other doctrine." 1ˢᵗ Timothy 1:3 (KJV)

"Who hath saved us, and called us with an holy calling, not according to our works, but according to His own purpose and grace, which was given us in Christ Jesus before the world was." 1ˢᵗ Timothy 2:9 (KJV)

We are not to teach, nor are we to hear any other doctrine other than that which is already taught, by the apostles, according to, St. John 17:20. (KJV)

Questions from the Author:

Now that you know the love of God: could you forgive yourself for having an abortion, or murder, child abuse or neglect, or any such thing, if so, by what process would you begin, and if not, why not?

Reflection:

_____

_____

_____

_____

_____

_____

_____

_____

_____

_____

_____

_____

_____

_____

_____

_____

_____

_____

_____

_____

CHAPTER IX

Was there a Verbal Command to be baptized

Was there any command to water baptize or to be water baptized? If so, who commanded it to be so, and are there other baptisms, if so, what were they? Is John the only Baptism, was John's baptism the last Baptist, or the first? What is Baptism?

Baptism is the immersing in water, and not only that if we are going to consider the thief on the cross as being buried with Jesus as baptism, or the Red sea crossing baptism where no one got wet, yet they were baptized, even Noah.

Meaning in the four square of the grave covered by liquid water or the clouds which is water.

The candidate for baptism must be immersed in water, meaning, buried as if dead and in the grave. Sprinkling does not cover the candidate, sprinkling water on the head or the feet is not baptism, to be baptized is to go into the water, and under the water rising again, as if being buried in the grave and resurrected like Jesus, and with Jesus. A person that is baptized is not only covered with water, but also does it in the name of the Lord Jesus Christ for the remission of sin. The speaking of the name Jesus applies the soap, or the cleansing substance to the candidate's sin while in the water.

This is the action of baptism

"...*Jesus went straightway up out of the water*," *Matthew 3:16(KJV)*

This tells us that He (Jesus) was completely immersed underwater.

"*Therefore we are buried with Him by baptism into death: that like as Christ was raised up from the dead by the glory of the Father, even so we also should walk in newness of life. But if we have been planted together in the likeness of His death, we shall be also in the likeness of His resurrection.*

Knowing this, that our old man is crucified with Him, that the body of sin might be destroyed, that henceforth we should not serve sin." *St. John 3:16 Romans 6:4 -6 (KJV)*

And Jesus, when He was baptized, went up, straightway out of the water: and, lo, the heavens were open unto Him, and He saw the spirit of God descending like a dove, and lighting upon Him." *Matthew 3:16. (KJV)*

Was there a Verbal Command to Baptize

There are many instances of baptism in the Bible: when Philip preached to the eunuch we saw the result of all the steps of salvation. We saw Philip teaching him from Isaiah 53.

We saw his response when he believed what Philip preached. The first part of his conversion was to hear the word of God. *Romans 10:14 (KJV)*

When he heard the word He asked the question what I must do to be saved.

The 2nd step was to believe through his faith what he had heard concerning: Christ death, burial and resurrection, his next step was to repent, then he asked what hinders me from being baptized?

And He was baptized in water, as we all must do. *Acts 8:12 (KJV)*

No verbal command to baptize or to be baptized per se

In the beginning there was no verbal command to baptize or to be baptized: however a subliminal command was given in the demonstration of baptism at the Red Sea crossing. No command was given to be baptized by Moses per se, but Moses and the children of Israel had to pass thru the Red Sea: which became their baptism.

The water was above them in the clouds, because the clouds are water, and the Sea rose-up as a wall of water on both sides of them, and they, the people, standing on the ground as we do while standing in the baptismal pool forming a square as a grave, we, going down into the water as a grave, being buried with Christ. However the bible said that the water congealed. Meaning to form the wall of water as crystals like ice. Meaning: Not actually getting wet. But in the sea and under the cloud, and water on each side. My Lord!

God said to Moses; *"but lift thou up thy rod, and stretch out thine hand over the Sea, and divide it: and the children of Israel shall go* **on dry ground through the midst of the Sea.**

And Moses stretched out his hand over the sea; and the Lord caused the sea to go back by a strong East wind all that night, and **made the Sea dry land**, *and the waters were divided.*

And the children of Israel went into the midst of the Sea upon the dry ground: and the waters were a wall unto them on their right hand, and on their left.

But the children of Israel walked upon dry land in the midst of the Sea; *and the waters were a wall unto them on their right hand, and on their left.*

No Verbal Command to Baptize or be Baptized

And with the blast of thy nostrils the waters were gathered together, the floods stood up-right as an heap, **and the depths were congealed in the heart of the Sea**." *Exodus 14:16, 21, 22, 29 Exodus 15:8 (KJV)*

Note this: this baptism also carries a man's name.

This is where we hear that this event is and was called Moses baptism unto this day.

*Moreover, brethren, I would not that you should be ignorant, how that all our fathers were under the cloud and all passed through the Sea; And **were all baptized unto Moses**, in the cloud and the Sea; And did all eat the same Spiritual meat;*

And did all drink the same spiritual drink: for they drank of that Spiritual Rock that followed them: and that Rock was Christ. 1ˢᵗ Corinthians 10: 1-4 (KJV)

Again, Noah was not commanded to be baptize persa nor to baptize, but he also was baptized, he and his whole house; as Moses and the children of Israel, passing through the Red Sea and Noah through the great flood.

"And God said unto Noah, the end of all flesh is come before me; for the earth is filled with violence through them; and behold, I will destroy them with the earth.

Make thee an Ark of Gopher wood;" Genesis 6:13-14 (KJV) **make yourself a way of escape**.

This was to save himself and his family as a way of salvation through this medium, this is representative of the church.

"And, behold, I, even I, do bring a flood of waters upon the earth, to destroy all flesh, wherein is the breath of life, from under the heaven; and everything that is in the earth shall die.

Notice that in each case of the Red Sea crossing, and the great flood it dwelt with water as a source of escape: (baptism) and in their escaping death, the natural salvation, that is, a man saving his house from natural destruction.

But with thee will I establish my covenant; and thou shalt come into the Ark, thou and thy sons, and thy wife, and thy son's wives with thee.

And of every living thing of all flesh, two of every sort shalt thou bring into the Ark, to keep them alive with thee; **they shall be male and female.***"* No bisexual or transgendered mentioned." *Genesis 6:17-19 (KJV)*

No Verbal Command to Baptize or be Baptized

"And the Lord said unto Noah, come thou and all thy house into the Ark; for thee have I seen righteous before me in this generation. And the flood was forty days upon the earth; and the waters increased, and bare up the Ark, and it was lifted up above the earth. And the waters prevailed, and were increased greatly upon the earth; and the Ark went upon the face of the waters. Genesis 7:1, 17-18 (KJV)

Which sometimes were disobedient, when once the long suffering of God waited in the days of Noah, while the Ark was a preparing, wherein few, that is, eight souls were saved by water. The male (Man) and his female (wife)

The like figure whereunto even doth now save us (not the putting away the filth of the flesh, but the answer of a good conscience toward God,) by the resurrection of Jesus Christ."
1ˢᵗ Peter 3:20-21 (KJV)

This is Noah's baptism, after this we have John's baptism:

After this we have John's baptism:

John preaching baptizing then Jesus

Then came John commanding everyone to repent, and to be baptized for the remission of sins,

John chapter 2, 3. After John went off the scene, Jesus took up **John's ministry** preaching John's gospel. Repent and **be baptized. Jesus ministry was to baptize with the Spirit, not with water.**

"After these things came Jesus and His disciples into the land of Judaea; and there He tarried with them, and baptized." St. John 3: 22 (KJV)

Jesus, according to St. John 3:22 (KJV) must have at some point baptized like Paul, even though Paul made his baptizing known only because of the division among the saints.

Other than that we may never have known that Paul had baptized any, for he stated that he was not sent to baptize, yet he baptized a few, all Paul was saying is that his ministry was not that of baptizing like John. Neither was Jesus here to baptize with water, He was here to baptize with the Holy Ghost.

*"Now I beseech you, brethren, by the name of our Lord Jesus Christ, that ye all speak the same thing, and that there be no divisions among you; but that you be perfectly joined together in the same mind and in the same judgment. (Oneness) For it hath been declared unto me of you, my brethren, by them which are of the house of Chloe, that there are contentions among you. Now this I say, that every one of you saith, I am of Paul; and I of Apollos; and I of Cephas; and I of Christ. Is Christ divided? Was Paul crucified for you? Or were you baptized in the name of Paul? I thank God that I baptized none of you, but Crispus and Gaius; lest any should say I had **baptized in my own name**. And I baptized also the household of Stephanas: besides. I know not whether I baptized any other. For Christ sent me not to baptize, but to preach the gospel: not with wisdom of words, lest the cross of Christ should be made of none effect." 1ST Corinthians 1:10-17 (KJV)*

All Paul was saying is, that baptizing was not his ministry as baptizing with water was not Jesus ministry, although Jesus taught the doctrine of baptism, and seemly may have baptized some. His baptism was to baptize with the Holy Spirit, which He never got to do with them because of their unbelief in Him as the son of God, or as God in the flesh. So Jesus ministry is yet unfulfilled with the Jews unto this day because of their unbelief.

John's Preaching then Jesus

Question put to Jesus

"Jesus answered and said unto him, verily, verily, I say unto thee. Except a man be born again, he cannot see the kingdom of God. Nicodemus said unto him, how can a man be born when he is old? Can he enter the second time into his mother's womb, and be born?"

Here we see **baptism** being associated with water in every instances, in the cloud and in the sea surrounded by (water.) Noah in the Ark also surrounded by water, John's baptism, and Jesus preaching baptism, immersing in water.

However these baptisms although current in their day, was demonstrations of things to come in our day, with the understanding that we all must be baptized in water, being covered by the water as the grave.

"Jesus answered, verily, verily, I say unto thee, except a man be born of water and of the spirit, he cannot enter into the kingdom of God. That which is born of the flesh is flesh; and that which is born of the Spirit is Spirit." St. John 3:3, 6 (KJV)

It seems that Moses may not have had any knowledge of baptism from the beginning, until they built the tabernacle, then he had to prepare a place for their washing, which was also representative of water baptism.

Questions from the Author:

Have you considered early morning prayer to begin your day, seating God at the forefront of your day. If not, why not?

Reflection:

_____

_____

_____

_____

_____

_____

_____

_____

_____

_____

_____

_____

_____

_____

_____

_____

_____

_____

_____

_____

_____

_____

_____

CHAPTER X

Apply the Name

Then came the apostles preaching and teaching the doctrine of repentance, and baptizing in the <u>NAME</u>.

Through all of the previous baptisms we had not heard the word, NAME, mentioned at all. Only the words: unto John and unto Moses, now the baptism must say: in the name of Jesus.

"Be it known unto you all, and to all the people of Israel, that by the name of Jesus Christ of Nazareth, whom ye crucified, whom God raised from the dead, even by Him doth this man stand here before you whole. This is the stone which was set at nought of you builders, which is become the head of the corner. Neither is there salvation in any other: for there is none other NAME under heaven given among men, whereby we must be saved." Acts 4:10-12 (KJV)

Here we see a man's name is required to be invoked into the process of salvation through baptism, after we have repented of our sins.

Matthew as one of the apostles; gave his point on baptism; which said.

"And Jesus came and spake unto them, saying, all power is given unto me in heaven and in earth. Go ye therefore, and teach all nations, baptizing them in the name of the Father, (Jesus) and of the son,(JESUS) and of the Holy Ghost. (JESUS) ⊗Matthew 28: 18-19 (KJV)

Matthew's Omissions

Here we hear the word name being invoked into the process, (with the misunderstanding of the word, name: when Matthew added the attributes of God. In the name of the Father, and of the son, and of the Holy Ghost.) Matthew's part or point was to tell them what to do, that is, to go and teach; and be baptized, without giving any other instruction. We know that there must have been more to the matter, but he didn't say preach, repent, believe, or new tongues someone else would give the understanding to the next point, or the next step on baptism with other steps added to the process.

Mark's gospel is No 2: it brings it in: and he said unto them, **Go ye into all the world, and preach,** (remember, Matthew only said to teach. he made no mention of preaching). But Mark added the second step that we must know as an extension to Matthews's gospel as steps to our salvation.

Apply the name

Matthew's Omission continues…

Then Mark brought in; **Go ye into all the world and preach to every creature**.

<u>Matthew omitted saying to preach at all, neither did he say to preach to everyone.</u>

Then Mark went on to say **"he that believeth and is baptized shall be saved**." but shall be saved. **He didn't say that you were saved:** *But he that believeth not shall be damned*.

Matthew didn't make a point to say, you must believe or be damned.

Here comes the promises that Matthew neglected to give unto us also.

"And these signs shall follow them that believe; Matthew gave no indication that there was more to be expected following the teaching, and repenting.

Then Mark said, "In **my NAME**". Not father, son and Holy Ghost: Not their names, but, **in my name** (One name only,) in my name comes the power, **they shall cast out devils; they shall speak with new tongues;**

They shall take up serpents; and if they drink any deadly thing, it shall not hurt them; they shall lay hands on the sick, and they shall recover." Mark 16:15-18. (KJV)

Matthew gave not a hint that there may be gifts or the power of miracles following.

Matthew didn't bring out these points, because he was only to initiate the process of baptism while others would complete the process. But somehow we got stalled at Matthew's gospel without checking what other writers had to say concerning this baptism process.

So we didn't complete the process of our salvation through the correct process of baptism. There are things others may not have mentioned, this is why we must search the scriptures for our answers.

Luke's gospel is No 3: Here comes Luke's gospel on baptism, and the resurrection, and the power which is the Holy Ghost, the comforter; which John's gospel preached, which we should receive.

These were the prophetic things which were to come.

Which in John's gospel Jesus promised to send in His name. It even said; **I will come to you.** This is personal to each individual.

Apply the Name

*"And I will pray the Father, and He shall give you another comforter that He may abide with you for ever;... But ye know Him; for He dwelleth with you, **and shall be in you.** I will not leave you comfortless: **I WILL COME TO YOU.***

*****But the comforter, which is the Holy Ghost**, whom the Father will send in my name, He shall teach you all things, and bring all things to your remembrance, whatsoever I have said unto you.*

At that day ye shall know that I am in my Father, and ye in me, and I in you." St. John 14: 16, 17, 26, 20 (KJV)

Luke's gospel No. 3 Luke's gospel mentions Christ suffering, and His resurrection on the third day, and that repentance and remission of sins should be preached in His name. (Not their names, as to say in the name of the Father, Son and Holy Ghost. These are the attributes of God not His name which we must bear.)

Beginning at Jerusalem, then they get a promise to be endued with power from on High, meaning the Holy Ghost, or the comforter.

The great commission:

"And he said unto them, These are the words which I spake unto you, while I was yet with you, that all things

*must be fulfilled, which was written in the Law of **Moses**, and in the **prophets**, and in the **psalms**, **concerning me**."*
Luke 24:44 (KJV)

These things are the prophecies spoken in time past of Jesus' death, burial and resurrection, which should come to pass. Unto us a child is born, unto us a son is given... etc.

"Then opened He their understanding, that they might understand the scriptures, And He said unto them, thus it is written, and thus it behoved Christ to suffer, and to rise from the dead the third day: And that repentance and remission of sins should be preached in His name among all nations, beginning at Jerusalem. And ye are witnesses, of these things.

And, behold, I send the promise of my Father upon you: but tarry ye in the city of Jerusalem, until ye be endued with power from on High. Luke 24: 44- 49 (KJV)

The Apostles Doctrine Applies the Name

Matthew didn't cover Mark's part of the great commission, neither did he mention Luke's first nor his second part concerning the great commission.

Neither did he cover Luke's second portion of the great commission which is found in the book of Acts. How is Luke's second part to the great commission located in the book of Acts?

Remember, it was Luke who wrote both the book of Luke, and continued it through the book of Acts; ending the Old Testament, transitioning into the New Testament.

This is the final step in the great commission;

Luke's second point to the great commission is:

"But ye shall receive power, after that the Holy Ghost is come upon you: and ye shall be witnesses unto me both in Jerusalem, and in all Judaea, and in Samaria, and unto the uttermost part of the world." Acts 1:8 (KJV)

Not In Jerusalem only, Judea and Samaria, but throughout the entire world.

Question:

Again, how did we manage to get stuck at Matthew's gospel on baptism, while all of this other information was available to us that we didn't properly complete the baptismal process?

It seems that we have misunderstood the message too long, and must now comply with that which we have heard and learned. Maybe it is because we did not know that there were four parts to the great commission, because of our unlearned teachers.

Now we see that the baptismal process is the same throughout the whole world for all people and denominations. So now we are without excuse. It is not totally the Pastor's reasonability to be concerned about our souls; we ourselves must be held accountable, and become active about learning what the scriptures have to say concerning our salvation as well as our lifestyle living, then ask questions. So we missed the fulness of our salvation in repentance, by not baptizing in Jesus name for the remission of sin, and receiving the gift of the Holy Ghost, because of improper doctrine and biblical misunderstanding. We totally missed the mark in this one. It is mandatory that we correct ourselves.

The Apostles Applies the Name

But it is not too late to correct ourselves, if we would put away our embarrassment; the tradition of men, and seek God in repentances to complete the process of our salvation: By using the Name of Jesus while being baptized in water again. We can no longer say "but my pastor doesn't do it like that" we are without excuse.

*"The former treaties have I made O Theophilus, **of all that Jesus began both to do and teach**,*

Until the day in which He was taken up, after that He through the Holy Ghost had given commandment unto the apostles whom He had chosen." Acts 1:1-2 (KJV)

The verbal command to be baptized

Now that the Apostles are on the scene; we have a verbal command: to be baptized in the name of the Lord Jesus Christ for the remission of sins.

Jesus is now crucified, and His blood has been released unto us: so now we have the substance for cleansing. We are now told to repent and be washed in the blood by faith, through baptism in applying His name. Jesus!

*"Then Peter said unto them, Repent, and be baptized every one of you **in the name of Jesus Christ** for the remission of sins, and ye shall receive the gift of the Holy Ghost." Acts 2:38(KJV)*

This is the day of Pentecost when the Church was born, bringing in the Holy Ghost, this day set precedent for the New Testament Church. **To the Jews first.**

"Repent ye therefore, and be converted, that your sins may be blotted out, when the times of refreshing shall come from the presence of the Lord;

*And He shall send Jesus Christ, **which before was preached unto you.**" Acts 3:19-20(KJV)*

"And now why tarriest thou? Arise, and be baptized, and wash away thy sins, calling on the name of the Lord." Acts 22:16 (KJV)

We are commanded to do all thing in His name.

These are the things which Jesus began both to do and teach, that our learning would now come from the Apostle's doctrine.

Remember: these are the same Apostles that Jesus prayed for in John's gospel in chapter 17:20. (KJV) Which said that we should learn of Him through their word.

The Apostles Applies His name

These are the same men which from their own teachings gave us the steps of salvation, which tells us that all of these men did agree that we; all as God's people coming into the same body of Christ must be partakers of the same word, and perform the same actions, such as, repent, and be baptized In the name of the Lord Jesus Christ. Our sins being remitted because of the blood of Jesus, the washing and His name, after that we must receive the gift of the Holy Ghost, with the utterance (which is speaking in tongues), which is the initial evidence tongue, which says to the one that is receiving the utterance that God now abides in their bodies. (Temple)

*"Neither pray I for these alone, but for them also which shall believe on me **through their word**." St. John 17:20-b (KJV)*

Here we see through the scripture that it is the Apostles that would teach us the scriptures concerning the doctrine of salvation, and the name of Jesus Christ.

Jesus never told us to learn of Himself through His word, but, to learn of Him through the words of His Apostles.

"And whatsoever ye do in word or deed, do all in the name of the Lord Jesus, giving thanks to God the Father by Him." Colossians 3:17 (KJV)

*"But when they believed Philip preaching the things concerning the kingdom of God, **and the name of Jesus Christ**, they were baptized, both men and women.*

Then Philip opened his mouth and began at the same scripture, and preached unto him, **Jesus**! *"And as they went on their way, they came unto a certain water: and the Eunuch said, see, here is water, what doeth hinder me to be baptized? And Philip said, if thou believeth with all thine heart, thou mayest. And he answered and said, I believe that **Jesus Christ is the son of God**. And he commanded the chariot to stand still: and they went down both into the water, both Philip and the Eunuch; and he baptized him." Acts 8:12 Acts 8:36-38 (KJV)*

These are the things which we must do and teach according to the scripture.

Hear this

"As I besought thee to abide still at Ephesus, when I went into Macedonia, that thou mightiest Charge some that they teach no other doctrine." 1st Timothy 1:3 (KJV)

The statement of the work of salvation is controversial, but there are some things that we must do as future members of the body of Christ in order to receive what Jesus has done for us.

The Work of Salvation

Question: is there works to our salvation?

The scriptures said:

"But God, who is rich in mercy, for His great love wherewith He love us.

Even when we were dead in sins, hath quickened us together with Christ, (by grace are you saved); And hath raised us up together, and made us sit together in heavenly places in Christ Jesus: That in ages to come He might shew the exceeding riches of His grace in His kindness toward us through Christ Jesus. For by grace are ye saved through faith; and that not of yourselves: it is the GIFT of God: Not of works." Ephesians 2: 4-9 (KJV)

What are works?

Works is the sacrifice which Jesus did at Calvary on man's behalf. Man couldn't do that particular work.

So what are we speaking about when we ask the question, is there works to our salvation?

This is the understanding:

Christ has performed all the work of salvation; now we must do the process of the work of salvation. What is the process part? The work of salvation is through the evangelism process.

Salvation is free to us, because we didn't have to pay the sin price, with the manual labor of death, but the process of works begins with hearing His word, and through faith, it causes us to believe what we have heard; concerning His death burial and resurrection.

After that: we complete this process of salvation by repenting of our sins, and being baptized in His name (**Jesus**), and receiving the gift of the Holy Ghost, and moving into Christian living, and maintaining good works.

Maintaining good works

We all must maintain good works. Maintaining good works is always necessary, even in general life; this isn't for the gentiles only, but for the Jews also as a demonstration to the world; that this is the way to live, and that it is good and prosperous, and peaceful to the soul. Because the time will come when we all will be in the same body, living a sanctified life, and standing before God to give account of our words and deed in this body.

"So then every one of us shall give account of himself to God." Romans 14:12 Matthew 12:36-37 (KJV)

"There is one body, and one spirit, even as ye are called in one hope of your calling;" Ephesians 4:4 (KJV)

Being warned of the Apostle Paul, that false prophets would arise; coming to us in sheep's clothing, but inwardly they are ravening wolves. But he also said that; ye shall know them by their fruits.

"Beware of false prophets, which come to you in sheep's clothing, but inwardly they are ravening wolves. Ye shall know them by their fruits, do men gather grapes of thorns, or figs of thistles? Matthew 7:15, 16 (KJV)

"Even so every good tree bringeth forth good fruit; but a corrupt tree bringeth forth evil fruit. A good tree cannot bring forth evil fruit, neither can a corrupt tree bring forth good fruit. Every tree that bringeth not forth good fruit is hewn down, and cast into the fire. Wherefore by their fruits ye shall know them. Matthew 7:17-20 (KJV)

Another passage of scripture which tells us about the difference between good and evil works, again.

For a good tree bringeth not forth corrupt fruit; neither doth a corrupt tree bringeth forth good fruit... Luke 6:43-45 (KJV)

Maintaining Good Works

And the word ministry is given for the perfecting of the saints that we may be able to walk in newness of life, while maintaining good works. This scripture said to us:

"That you might walk worthy of the Lord unto all pleasing, being fruitful in every good work, and increasing in the knowledge of God:

Walk worthy of the Lord. Living a life worthy of the Lord. Which results in, fruitfulness, and increased knowledge of God's strength to endure

(Verse 11). And thankfulness (12) made us fit, qualified us.

Giving thanks unto the Father, which has made us meet to be partakers of the inheritance of the saints in light:" Colossian 1:10-12 (KJV)

These are our good works?

"Jesus said; but I say unto you which hear: Love your enemies, do good to them which hate you, Bless them that curse you, and pray for them that despitefully use you. And him that smiteth thee on the one cheek offer him the other. And him that taketh away the cloak forbid not to take away the coat also. Give to every man that asketh of thee; and of him that taketh away thy goods ask them not again. And as ye would that men should do to you, do ye also to them likewise. For if you love them which love you, what thank

have ye? For sinners also love those that love them. And if ye do good to them which do good to you, what thank have ye? For sinners also do even the same. And if ye lend to them of whom ye hope to receive, what thank have ye? For sinners also lend to sinners, to receive as much again.

But love ye your enemies, and do good, and lend, hoping for nothing again; and your reward shall be great, and ye shall be the children of the Highest: for He is kind unto the unthankful and to the evil. Judge not, and ye shall not be judged: condemn not, and ye shall not be condemned: forgive, and ye shall be forgiven: Be therefore merciful, for your Father is also merciful.

Give, and it shall be given unto you; good measure, pressed down, and shaken together, and running over, shall men give into your bosom. For with the same measure that ye mete withal it shall be measured to you again." Luke 6:27-38

Back to the word ministry in maintaining good works.

"I Therefore, the prisoner of the Lord, beseech you that ye walk worthy of the vocation wherein ye are called,

With all lowliness and meekness, with longsuffering, forbearing one another in love;

Endeavoring to keep the unity of the spirit in the bond of peace." Ephesians 4:1-3 (KJV)

There is much instruction given to the saints, because the devil is gone out into the world to deceive you. Paul said; false prophets, Beware, be not deceived.

Check this out

"For such are false apostles, deceitful workers, transforming themselves into the apostles of Christ.

And no marvel; Satan himself is transformed into an angel of light.

Therefore it is no great thing if his ministers also be transformed as the ministers of righteousness; whose end shall be according to their works." 2ⁿᵈ Corinthians 11:13-15 (KJV)

Questions from the Author:

Now that you may understand sin better; how can you cause one soul to abandon sin, and could your lifestyle become their lifeline unto salvation?

Reflection:

_____

_____

_____

_____

_____

_____

_____

_____

_____

_____

_____

_____

_____

_____

_____

_____

_____

_____

_____

_____

CHAPTER XI

The Subject of Faith

Why do we need faith? Because it is necessary to have faith in order to please God according to the scriptures. And every person must understand that their salvation is contingent upon their faith in the redemptive process, which begins and ends with the sacrifice of Jesus Christ.

Question: You may ask the question; what is faith? Just to put it in a simplified form:

(Faith is the engine that drives the actions being performed, which is a word spoken, spiritually or naturally: even sinners have faith in what they attempt to accomplish.) Refer to Hebrews 11:6 (KJV)

But there are different kinds of faith; there is the measure of faith, which is given to every man, even sinners. There is mustard seed faith. The God kind of faith. The faith that groweth. Grace is of the faith of God. And the command to have faith in God. That which is not of faith. Let us look at a few scriptures on faith, and their importance.

Purpose for Faith:

*"We are bound to thank God always for you, brethren, as it is meet, because that your **faith groweth exceedingly**, and the charity of every one of you all toward each other aboundeth; So that we ourselves glory in you in the churches of God for your **patience and faith in all your persecutions and tribulations that ye endure:** Which is a manifest token of the righteous judgement of God, that ye may be counted worthy of the kingdom of God, for which ye also suffer:"* 2 Thessalonians 1:3-5(KJV)

*"**Therefore it is of faith that it might be by grace**; to the end the promise might be sure to all the seed; not to that only which is of the law, but to that also which **is of the faith of Abraham**; who is the father of us all."* Romans 4:16(KJV)

*"And Jesus answering saith unto them, **Have faith in God**."* Mark 11:22; (KJV)

"And he that doubteth is damned, if he eateth, because he eateth not of faith: for whatsoever is not of faith is sin." Romans 14:23 (Romans 12:3; Matthew 17:20) (KJV)

The power of faith saves and glorifies God:

"And it came to pass, as He was come nigh unto Jericho, a certain blind man sat by the way side begging: And hearing the multitude pass by, he asked what it meant. And they told him, that Jesus of Nazareth passeth by. And he cried, saying,

*Jesus, thou son of David, have mercy on me. And they which went before rebuked him, that he should hold his peace: but he cried so much the more, Thou son of David, have mercy on me. And Jesus stood, and commanded him to be brought unto Him: and when he was come near, He asked him, Saying, what wilt thou that I should do unto thee? And he said, Lord, that I may receive my sight. And Jesus said unto him, receive thy sight: **thy faith hath saved thee.** And immediately he received his sight, and followed Him, glorifying God: and all the people, when they saw it, gave praise unto God."* Luke 18:35-43 (KJV)*

Faith purifies the heart

"And put no difference between us and them, purifying their hearts by faith." Acts 15:9 (KJV)

Faith to be healed

*"And there sat a certain man at Lystra, impotent in his feet, being a cripple from his mother's womb, who never had walked: The same heard Paul speak: who steadfastly beholding him, and perceiving **that he had faith to be healed,** Said with a loud voice, stand upright on thy feet. And he leaped and walked." Acts 14:8-10 (KJV)*

Faith justifies

"Therefore being justified by faith, we have peace with God through our Lord Jesus Christ. By whom also we have

access by faith into His grace wherein we stand, and rejoice in hope of the glory of God." Romans 5:1, 2 (KJV)

The Shield of faith

"Above all, taking the shield of faith, wherewith ye shall be able to quench all the fiery darts of the wicked." Ephesian 6:16(KJV)

Operation of His Faith

"Buried with Him in baptism, wherein also ye are risen with him through the faith of the operation of God, who hath raised Him from the dead." Colossians 2:12 (KJV)

The Purpose for the word gifts

For the perfecting of the saints, for the work of the ministry, for the edifying of the body of Christ:

This brings us back to the Apostles, and Prophets, Evangelist, Pastors and Teachers of God: who must continue to teach and preach this message of Jesus's, salvation, repentance, sanctification and holiness repetitiously.

"As I besought thee to abide still at Ephesus, when I went to Macedonia, that thou mightiest charge some that they teach no other doctrine." 1ˢᵗ *Timothy 1:3* **(KJV)**

And how long must we hear this message?

*"Till we all come in the **unity of the faith**, and of the knowledge of the son of God, unto a perfect man, unto the measure of the stature of the fulness of Christ: That we henceforth be no more children, tossed to and fro, and carried about with every wind of doctrine, by the sleight of men, and cunning craftiness, whereby they lie in wait to deceive; But speaking the truth in love, may grow up into Him in all things, which is the head, even Christ: From whom the whole body fitly joined together and compacted by that which every joint supplieth, according to the effectual working in the measure of every part, maketh increase of the body into edifying of itself in love." Ephesians 4:11-16 (KJV)*

Discovering His mysteries

In our receiving of the doctrine of the Apostles we discover the hidden things which Christ would have us to know for our learning, and for the perfecting of the saints.

"That their hearts might be comforted, being knit together in love, and unto all riches of the full assurance of understanding, to the <u>acknowledgement of the mystery of God,</u> And of the Father, and of Christ; In whom are hid all the treasures of wisdom and knowledge." Colossians 2: 2, 3 (KJV)

"For we are members of His body, of His flesh, and of His bones. For this cause shall a man leave his father and mother, and shall be joined unto his wife, and they two shall be one flesh,

This is a great mystery: but I speak concerning Christ (the male) and (the female) the church.

Nevertheless let every one of you in particular so love his wife even as himself (the man); and the wife (the woman) see that she reverence her husband. Ephesians 5:30-33 (KJV)

So ought men (male) to love their wives (female) as their own bodies. He that loveth his wife (female) loveth himself.

For no man ever yet hateth his own flesh; but nourisheth and cherisheth it, even as the Lord the Church." Ephesians 5:28-29 (KJV)

These are ensample of the mysteries which the body of Christ have not known, nor understood as perfecting the saints through the steps of salvation.

The purpose for being the church

Carrying out the church's' purpose

The ministry of the church is conceived by God, and initiated through the Apostles, acting under Jesus' authority. Paul admonished the church at Corinth to do things "in a decent and orderly way.

"He said to them: Let all things be done decently and in order." 1ˢᵗ Corinthians 14:40 (KJV)

The New Testament church is unlike the wilderness church; where only the Jews were a part of the functioning's of God, unless you happened to be one who had proselyted themselves unto the Jews, according to the scriptures, Which said:

"These twelve Jesus sent forth, and commanded them, saying, go not into the way of the gentiles, and into any city of the Samaritans enter ye not: But go rather to the lost sheep of the house of Israel. And as ye go, preach..." Matthew 10: 5-7 (KJV)

Finally

The New Testament church would recognize no racial, sexual, political or geographical boundaries in its functioning, but a new tenet would be put into place for all, that is, the simple steps of salvation: after His death burial and resurrection. But now, he saith,

"For this is my blood of the New Testament, which is shed for many for the remission of sins. According to the scriptures:" Matthew 26:28 (KJV)

"For ye are all the children of God by faith in Christ Jesus. For as many of you as have been baptized into Christ have put on Christ. There is neither Jew nor Greek, there is neither bond nor free, there is neither male nor female: for ye are all one in Christ Jesus. Galatians 3:26-28 (KJV)

The functions of the New Testament church are these, and must be implemented by the bishops, elders, or oversees as they are named in the local church; as have been required by the scriptures which saith that they are to:

"*Take heed therefore unto yourselves, and to all the flock, over the which the Holy Ghost hath made you overseers, to feed the church of God, which He hath purchased with His own blood.*" Acts 20:28 (KJV)

These should be the functions of the church being carried out by the local church assemblies around the world. Not denominationally.

Some people are appointed to service: Paul said that he was appointed to this work

"*Whereunto* **I am appointed a preacher**, *and an apostle, and a teacher of the gentiles.*" 2nd Timothy 1:11(KJV)

"*That no man should be moved by these afflictions: for yourselves know that we are appointed thereunto.*" 1st. Thessalonians 3:3(KJV)

"*And I said, what shall I do, Lord? And the Lord said unto me, Arise, and go into Damascus; and there it shall be told thee of all* **things which are appointed for thee to do**." Acts 22:10 (KJV)

"*And hath made of one blood all nations of men for to dwell on all the face of the earth, and hath determined the times* **before appointed**, *and the bounds of their habitation;* **Because He hath appointed a day**, *in the which He will* *judge the world in righteousness by that man whom He hath ordained; whereof He hath given assurance unto all men, in that He hath raised Him from the dead." Acts 17:26, 31(KJV)*

*"**For God hath not appointed us to wrath**, but to obtain salvation by our Lord Jesus Christ, Who died for us, that, whether we wake or sleep, we should live together with Him..." 1 Thessalonians 5:9-10 (KJV)*

These things the church must do.

A. To glorify Christ: *"husband (Male), love your wives (Female), even as Christ loved the church, and gave Himself for it; That He might sanctify and cleanse it with the washing of water by the word, that He might present it to Himself a glorious church, not having spot, or wrinkle, or any such thing; but it should be holy and without blemish." Ephesians 5:25-27(KJV)*

"For ye are bought with a price: therefore glorify God in your body, and in your spirit, which are God's;" 1st Corinthians 6:20 (KJV)

B. To worship God in spirit and in truth: *"having therefore, brethren, boldness to enter into the holiest by the blood of Jesus, By a new and living way, which He hath consecrated for us, through the veil, that is to say, His flesh; And having an High Priest over the house of God; Let us draw near with a true heart in full assurance of faith, having our hearts sprinkled from an evil conscience, and our bodies* *washed with pure water. Let us hold fast the profession of our faith without wavering; (for He is faithful that promised And let us consider one another to provoke unto love and to good works: Not forsaking the assembling of ourselves together, as the matter of some is; but exhorting one another: and so much the more, as ye see the day approaching." Hebrews 10: 19-25 (KJV)*

C. **To preach the gospel**: *"Moreover, brethren, I declare unto you the gospel which I preached unto you, which also ye have received, and wherein ye stand; By which also **ye are saved, if ye keep in memory what I preached unto you, unless ye have believed in vain**. For I delivered unto you first of all that which I also received, how that Christ died for our sins according to the scriptures;*

And that He was buried, and that He rose again the third day according to the scriptures: and that He was seen of Cephas, then of the twelve: After that, HE was seen of above five hundred brethren at once; of whom the greater part remain unto this present, but some are fallen asleep.

After that He was seen of James: then all of the apostles. And last of all He was seen of me also, as of one born out of due time. For I am the least of the apostles, that am not meet to be called an apostle, because I persecuted the church of God. But by the grace of God I am what I am: and His grace which was bestowed upon me was not in vain; but I labored more abundantly than they all: yet not I, but the grace of God which was in me. Therefore whether it were I or they, so we preach, and so ye believed." 1ˢᵗ Corinthians 15:1-11 (KJV)

D. To observe the sacraments of baptism and the Lords supper. *1ˢᵗ Corinthians 11 (KJV)*

E. To supply instruction in righteousness: *"and He gave some, apostles; and some, prophets: and some, evangelist; and some, pastors; and some, teachers;*

For the perfection of the saints, *for the work of the ministry, for the edifying of the body of Christ: till we all come in the unity of the faith, and of the knowledge of the Son of God, unto a perfect man, unto the measure of the stature of the fullness of Christ*

F. To exercise discipline: *"now we command you, brethren, in the name of our Lord Jesus Christ, that ye withdraw yourselves from every brother that walketh disorderly, and not after the tradition of which he received of us. For yourselves know how ye ought to follow us: for we behaved not ourselves disorderly among you; Neither did we eat any man's bread for nought; but wrought with labour and travail night and day, that we might not be chargeable to any of you; Not because we have not power, but to make ourselves an ensample unto you to follow us. For even when we were with you, this we commanded you, that if any would not work, neither should he eat. For we hear that there are some which walk among you disorderly, working not at all, but are busybodies. Now them that are such we command and exhort by our Lord Jesus Christ, that with quietness they work, and* *eat their own bread. But ye, brethren, be not weary in well doing. But ye, brethren, be not weary in well doing. And if any man obey not our word by this epistle, note that man, and have no company with him, that he may be ashamed. Yet count him not as an enemy, but admonish him as a brother." II Thessalonians 3: 6-15 (KJV)*

G. to provide fellowship and spiritual growth:

"As you know how we exhorted and comforted and charged every one of you, as a father doth his children, That ye would walk worthy of God, who hath called you into

His kingdom and glory. For this cause also thank we God without ceasing, because, when ye received the word of God which ye heard of us, ye received it not as the word of men, but as it is in truth, the word of God, which effectually worketh also in you that believe." 1st Thessalonians 2:11-13(KJV)

"We then that are strong ought to bear the infirmities of the weak, and not to please ourselves. Let every one of us please his neighbor for his good to edification.

For even Christ pleased not Himself; but, as it is written, the reproaches of them that reproached thee fell on me.

For whatsoever things were written aforetime were written for our learning, that we through patience and comfort of the scriptures might have hope.

Now the God of patience and consolation grant you to be likeminded one toward another according to Christ Jesus: That ye with one mind and one mouth glorify God, even the Father of our Lord Jesus Christ. Wherefore receive ye one another, as Christ also received us to the glory of God." Romans 15:1-7(KJV)

"For He is our peace, who hath made both one, and hath broken down the middle wall of partition between us.

Having abolished in His flesh the enmity, even the law of commandments contained in ordinances; for to make in Himself of twain one new man, so making peace; And that He might reconcile both unto God in one body by the cross, having slain the enmity thereby: And came and preached peace to you which were afar off, and to them that were nigh. For through Him we both have access by one spirit unto the Father. Now therefore ye are no more strangers and foreigners, but fellowcitizens with the saints, and of the household of God; And are built upon the foundation of the apostles and prophets, Jesus Christ being the chief corner stone; In whom all the building fitly framed together groweth unto an holy temple in the Lord: In whom ye also are builded together for an habitation of God through the spirit." Ephesians 2:14-22 (KJV)

"To minister to the unfortunate, *"with food as well as with healing miracles: pure religion and undefiled before God and the Father is this, to visit the fatherless and widows* *in their affliction, and to keep himself unspotted from the world." James 1:27(KJV)*

"And in those days, when the number of the disciples was multiplied, there arose a murmuring of the Grecians against the Hebrews, because their widows were neglected in the daily ministration.

Then the twelve called the multitude of the disciples unto them, and said, it is not reason that we should leave the word of God, and serve tables. Wherefore, brethren, look ye out among you seven men of honest report, full of the Holy Ghost and wisdom, whom we may appoint over this business. But we will give ourselves continually to prayer, and to the ministry of the word. And the saying pleased the whole multitude: and they chose Stephen, a man full of faith and of the Holy Ghost, and Philip, and Prochorus, and Nicanor, and Timon, and Parmenas, and Nicolas a Proselyte of Antioch: Whom they set before the apostles: and when they had prayed, they laid their hands on them." Acts 6: 1-7 (KJV)

To promote Christian unity: *"now I beseech you, brethren, by the name of our Lord Jesus Christ, that ye all speak the same thing, and that there be no division among you; but that you be perfectly joined together in the same mind and in the same judgment." 1ˢᵗ Corinthians 1: 10(KJV)*

"Let us therefore follow after the things which make for peace, and things wherewith one may edify one another. But why dost thou judge thy brother? Or why dost thou

set at nought thy brother? For we shall all stand before the judgment seat of Christ." Romans 14: 19; 10 (KJV)

The church is a place for evangelism, we must make Christ and the church our centerpiece of our world.

Questions from the Author:

Is life better at this stage of your life, or are there situations that you have not dealt with that are impeding you progress in life, if so, what is your remedy to move forward? will you try to solve the problem on your own, or will you seek spiritual counsel?

Reflection:

_____

_____

_____

_____

_____

_____

_____

_____

_____

_____

_____

_____

_____

_____

_____

_____

_____

_____

_____

CHAPTER XII

Becoming Messengers of Christ for Christ

The fundamental doctrine of salvation is not about the need to be saved only; and the steps to salvation in order to be saved. It is about Christian living and maintaining good works after one has been saved: but we as Christians must also become the same messengers of salvation that was ministered to us. This documentary of the doctrine of salvation covers a continuation of the salvation process until salvation is accomplished in all that will come, and until the end of this dispensation, and for all that will come afterward.

Example

"One of the two which heard John speak, and followed him, was Andrew, Simon Peter's brother. He first findeth his own brother Simon, and saith to him, we have found the Messiah, which is, being interpreted, the Christ. And he brought him to Jesus. And when Jesus beheld him, He said, thou art Simon the son of Jona: thou shall be called Cephas, which is by interpretation, a stone." John 1:40-42 (KJV)

The woman then left her waterpot, and went her way into the city, and saith to men, Come, see a man, which told me all things that I ever did: is this not the Christ?" St. John 4:28-29 (KJV)

Andrew introduced his brother Peter to Jesus the saviour, and before Peter received his fellowship and salvation from Jesus, Jesus spoke his future to him. Then the Samaritan woman also introduced her ex-lovers to Christ.

"And I say also unto thee, that thou art Peter, and upon this rock I will build my church; and the gates of hell shall not prevail against it." Matthew 16:18 (KJV)

The saying of today concerning salvation is, reach one, and teach one.

The apostle's doctrine and the minister are there for the perfecting of the saints; once they have been born through the Spirit of God, as Jesus stated to Nicodemus.

"Jesus answered and said unto him, verily, verily, I say unto thee, except a man be born again, he cannot see the kingdom of God. Jesus answered, verily, verily, I say unto thee, except a man be born of water and of the Spirit, he cannot enter into the kingdom of God." St. John 3:3, 5(KJV)

"Not by works of righteousness which we have done, but according to His mercy He saved us, by the washing of regeneration, and renewing of the Holy Ghost. Which He

shed on us abundantly through Jesus Christ our saviour."
Titus 3: 5-6 (KJV)

Concerning the Leadership in the Church

It is imperative that we cause others to be saved by the word of God, our Christian living and our good works as an example to others by our love one to another.

Stephen and Job; high moral standards

Stephen and Job are perfect examples of what a Holy Ghost: God fearing man looks like, and should be. God used others in time past, which had great flaws in their character to build and take part in the leadership of building the ministry. Such as, Moses as a killer, David as a murderer, and a man of lust; his son Solomon, as a womanizer. Paul as a persecutor of the Christians, Adam's disobedient; Abraham, lustful and succumbing to his wife's voice and his flesh. But Stephen and Job: seems to be the true model of what the church leadership must be, faithful in the fear of God, with High moral standards. The Husband (Male) of one wife (Female), without a bad reputation, but full of the Holy Ghost, and his house being in subjection to the leadership

High Moral standards in the body of Christ

"If be so that ye have heard Him, and have been taught by Him, as the truth is in Jesus: That ye put off concerning the former conversation the old man, which is corrupt according to the deceitful lusts; And be renewed in the Spirit of your mind; And that ye put on the new man, which after God is created in righteousness and true holiness.

Wherefore putting away lying, speak every man truth with his neighbor: for we are members one to another. Be ye angry, and sin not: let not the sun go down upon your wrath: Neither give place to the devil. Let him that stole steal no more: but rather let him labour, working with his hands the things which is good, that he may have to give to him that needeth. Let no corrupt communication proceed out of your mouth, but that which is good to the use of edifying, that it may minister grace unto the hears. And grieve not the Holy Spirit of God, whereby ye are sealed unto the day of His redemption. Let all bitterness, and wrath, and anger, and clamour, and evil speaking, be put away from you, with all malice. And be ye kind one to another, tenderhearted, forgiving one another, even as God for Christ sake hath forgiven you." Ephesians 4: 21-32 (KJV)

"Be ye therefore followers of God, as dear children; And walk in love, as Christ also hath loved us, and hath given Himself for us an offering and a sacrifice to God for a sweetsmelling savour. Endeavoring to keep the unity of the Spirit in the bond of peace." Ephesians 5:1-3 (KJV)

Summary of verse three:

We as the church are to use the example of the Good Samaritan. The leadership in the house of God must be well rounded: "*Blameless, in the world and in the church, and of a good report. **The husband (Male) of one wife (Female)**; not polygamy or other outside interest, like Solomon. Vigilant: meaning alert, **watchful**: Attentive. Sober: must be of sound mind, **self-controlled:** temperate, and discreet. **Of good behaviour**: of good character, **trustworthy:** grounded, of a good moral sense. **Given to hospitality**, he must have love and support of strangers. **Apt to teach:** he must be a teacher of good things, give instruction in the word, rightly dividing the word of truth.*

*   **Not given to wine:** he must not tarry at the wine, a brawler, living in the effects of wine, fighting. **No striker:** He must not be a fighter, or bully. **Not greedy of filthy lucre:** he must not be greedy for money, eager to be wealthy, ill-gotten gain. **But patient:** he must also be patient with people, patient in waiting for change, and patient in persecutions. **Not a brawler:** one that is a Carouser, loud, fight. **Not covetous:** he must never have a fixed lustful passion upon the things of others, whether they are good or bad. One that ruleth well his own house, having his children with all gravity. (For if a man know not how to rule his own house, how shall he take care of the house of God?) **Not a novice,** lest he being lifted up with pride he fall into the condemnation of the devil. Moreover he must have a good*

report of them which are without least he fall into reproach and the snare of the devil." 1ˢᵗ *Timothy 3:1-7 (KJV)*

Carry-over from Timothy to Titus:

"Instruction is given to Timothy, and to Titus as to how to oversee the house of God, and how the Christians once saved, and grown in age and in the knowledge of Christ must be able to be an excellent example to the younger saints and the outsiders looking in: watching the lifestyles of the church; having nothing negative to speak against the house and the people of God. All the apostles, and preachers were given the same message

For this cause left I thee in Crete, that thou shouldest set in order the things that are wanting, and ordain elders in every city, as I had appointed thee: If any man be blameless, the husband of one wife, having faithful children not accused of riot or unruly. For a bishop (the pastor or elder) *must be blameless, as the steward of God; not selfwilled, not soon angry, not given to wine no striker, not given to filthy lucre; But a lover of hospitality, a lover of good men, sober, just, holy, temperate; Holding fast the faithful word as he hath been taught, that he may be able by sound doctrine both to exhort and to convince the gainsayers."* Titus 1:5-9 (KJV)

Standards for the Aged men in the church

"But speak thou the things which becometh sound doctrine: That the aged men be sober, grave, temperate, and sound in faith, in charity, in patience

Standards for the aged women in the church

The aged women likewise, that they be in behaviour as becometh holiness, not false accusers, not given to much wine, teachers of good things; That they may teach the young women to be sober, to love their husbands, to love their children, Discreet, chaste, keepers at home, obedient to their own husbands, that the word of God be not blasphemed."
Titus 2: 1-5 (KJV)

Young men a good pattern

Young males are not exempt from holiness, sound doctrine, sound speech, young men likewise exhort to be sober minded. *"In all things shewing thyself a pattern of good works: in doctrine shewing uncorruptness, gravity, sincerity. Sound speech that cannot be condemned; that he that is of the contrary part may be ashamed, having no evil thing to say of you. Exhort servants to be obedient to their own masters, and to please them well in all things; not answering again; not purloining, but showing all good fidelity; that they may adorn the doctrine of God our Saviour in all things. For the grace of God that bringeth salvation hath appeared to all men. Teaching us that, denying ungodliness and worldly lust, we should soberly, righteously, and godly in this present world; reputation, good works, leadership and growth in the knowledge of Christ.*

Looking for that blessed hope, and the glorious appearing of the great God and our Saviour Jesus **Christ;** *Who gave Himself for us, that He might redeem us from all iniquity, and purify unto Himself a peculiar people, zealous of good works.* These things speak, *and exhort, and rebuke with all authority. Let no man despise thee." Titus 2:6-15 (KJV)*

Judge not those that are without:

The book of Titus reminds us of our past, that we don't harshly judge those that are walking in our old shoes.

"Put them in mind to be subject to principalities and powers, to obey magistrates, to be ready to every good work,

To speak evil of no man, to be no brawlers, but gentle, showing all meekness unto all men. For we ourselves also were sometimes foolish, disobedient, deceived, serving divers' lusts and pleasures, living in malice and envy, hateful, and hating one another.

But after that the kindness and love of God our saviour toward man appeared, Not by works of righteousness which we have done, but according to His mercy He saved us, by the washing of regeneration, and renewing of the Holy Ghost; Which He shed on us abundantly through Jesus Christ our Saviour; That being justified by His grace, we should be made heirs according to the hope of eternal life. This is a faithful saying, and these things I will that thou affirm constantly, that they which have believed in God might be careful to maintain good works. These things are good and profitable unto men." Titus 3:1-11

Again, we are too see our former ungodly selves in others, and allow the compassion to flow, and judge not those that are without.

"And such were some of you: but ye are washed, but ye are sanctified, but ye are justified in the name of the Lord Jesus, and by the spirit of our God." 1ˢᵗ Corinthians 6:11 (KJV)

"But now I have written unto you not to keep company, if any man that is called a brother be a fornicator, or covetous, or an idolater, or a railer, or a drunkard, or an extortioners; with such an one no not to eat. For what have I to do to judge them also that are without? Do not ye judge them that are within? But them that are without God judgeth.

Therefore put away from among yourselves that wicked person." 1ˢᵗ Corinthians 5:11-13 (KJV)

It is plain that the saints are to become and remain a separate entity from the world. Professing a holy lifestyle before men and in the Church. Gods' church.

Duties of the Church, in holiness

"I exhort therefore, that, first of all, supplications, prayers, intercessions, and giving of thanks, be made for all men.

For kings, and for all that are in authority; that we may lead a quiet and peaceable life in all godliness and honesty.

For this is good and acceptable in the sight of God our Saviour; who will men to be saved, and to come into the knowledge of the truth.

For there is one God, and one mediator between God and men, the man Christ Jesus.

Who gave Himself a ransom for all, to be testified in due time.

Whereunto I am ordained a preacher, and an apostle, (I speak the truth in Christ, and lie not ;) a teacher of the gentiles in faith and verity.

I will therefore that men pray everywhere, lifting up holy hands, without wrath and doubting. In like manner also, the women adorn themselves in modest apparel, with shamefacedness and sobriety; not with broided hair, or gold, or pearls, or costly array;

But (which becometh women professing godliness) with good works." 1ˢᵗ Timothy 2:1-10 (KJV)

Questions from the Author:

Have you considered love as an healing agent, do you remember God's love as Calvary? If so, will you use it?

Reflection:

_____

_____

_____

_____

_____

_____

_____

_____

_____

_____

_____

_____

_____

_____

_____

_____

_____

_____

_____

_____

_____

CHAPTER XIII

Concerning unity in the church

**High moral standards in the church continues'"
Unity is the requirement**

The church should be in unity as one, speaking and having the same knowledge and revelation of who God is in Jesus, and His purpose for man. And in the fulness of the knowledge of Christ which Paul received: Knowing the mysteries of God, which we should receive growing up into the fulness of the stature and knowledge of Christ after His own will: being a perfected man. Living in His revealed glory, and the wonders of His manifested power, and of His revealed prophecies, His revealed glory, being full of His wisdom and understanding, and walking in the light of His manifest glory. These things belong to us, according to His will.

"Now we have received, not the spirit of the world, but the spirit which is of God; that we might know the things that are freely given to us of God." 1ˢᵗ Corinthians1:12(KJV)

"He that spared not His own son, but delivered Him up for us all, how shall He not with Him also freely give us all things?" Romans 8:32 (KJV)

"such as one was caught up to the third heaven.

And heard things that all men of God should know, as the sons of God. How that he was caught up into paradise, and heard unspeakable words, which is not lawful for a man to utter." 2Corinthians 12:2, 4 (KJV)

We find that in creation that all things work together, in its own place, time, and season in order to be in perfect unity, harmonized being unified in nature. The same principles apply to the body of Christ.

"Again I say unto you, that if two of you shall agree on earth as touching anything that they shall ask, it shall be done for them of my Father which is in heaven. For where two or three are gathered together in my name, there am I in the midst of them." Matthew 18:19-20 (KJV)

The church, the body of Christ is commanded to be one unified body, fitly joined together

"From whom the whole body fitly joined together and compacted by that which every joint supplieth, according to the effectual working in the measure of every part, which maketh increase of the body unto the edifying of itself in love." Ephesians 4:16 (KJV)

Unity is the Requirement

This spirit not many of us have, because of false doctrine, denominational teachings, and suppression of Christ by the letter of the law. In the Psalms David said, that it is good for brethren to dwell together in unity, Psalms 133:1 (KJV)

In another place it tells us to entertain strangers, so the church is supposed to be visible in all places. Hebrews 13:1-2 (KJV)

The Responsibilities of the church

In the Church: there are some obligations that should be undertaken by certain saints, to support, promote, and uphold the operations of the activities of the church. The responsibility of certain others that is to wait on tables (that is to ministrate) to provide to the members the things that are lacking outside of the pastoral duties in order to accomplish this; these must have certain qualifications, as described in verse three, having successfully passed through the salvation process, being qualified to serve. Deacons

Proof of Ministrative duties in the church

"And in those days, when the number of the disciples was multiplied, there arose a murmuring of the Grecians against the Hebrews, because their widows were being neglected.

This gives us the examples of duties to widows, and not to be undertaken by the pastors, but by others.

Then the twelve called the multitude of the disciples unto them, and said, It is not reason that we should leave the word

of God, and serve tables. Wherefore, brethren, look ye out among you seven men of honest report, full of the Holy Ghost and wisdom, whom we may appoint over this business. But we will give ourselves continually to prayer, and to the work of the ministry. And the saying pleased the whole multitude: and they chose Stephen, a man full of faith and of the Holy Ghost, and Philip, and Prochorus, and Nicanor, and Timon, and Parmenas, and Nicolas a proselyte of Antioch: Whom they set before the apostles: and when they had prayed, they laid their hands on them. And the word of God increased; and the number of the disciples multiplied in Jerusalem greatly; and a great company of the priest were obedient to the faith. And Stephen, full of faith and power, did great wonders and miracles among the people." Acts 6: 1-8 (KJV)

Family education:

This is a duty of the church teachers: to teach growth and corrective discipline to children, and self. We are told not to provoke our children to wrath, the scriptures said that we were to:

"Train up a child in the way that he should go: and when he is old, he will not depart from it." Proverbs 22:6(KJV)

"And, ye fathers, provoke not your children to wrath: but bring them up in the nurture and admonition of the Lord." Ephesian 6:4(KJV)

The Responsibilities of the Church

Proof of ministrative duties in the church continues…

Altar workers:

Surely there must be Altar workers, it was said to have been reported in the Law of Moses, because of 1st Corinthians chapter 9. Which saith:

"Do ye not know that they which minister about holy things live of the things of the Temple? And they which wait at the altar are partakers with the altar?"
1st Corinthians 9:13 (KJV)

Mentorship:

Naomi mentored Ruth in the word, and the deity and the ways of her God; and as Mordecai mentored Esther. After Naomi's husband and sons were dead; Naomi saw fit to return to her home in Judah, and she made an attempt to send her daughter in-laws back to their homeland: while Orpah consented to return to her heathen country; Ruth thought to remain with Naomi her mother in-law.

"And they lifted up their voice, and wept again: and Orpah kissed her mother in law; but Ruth clave unto her. And she said, behold, thy sister in law is gone back unto her people, and unto her gods: return thou after thy sister in law.

And Ruth said, Intreat me not to leave thee, or to return from following after thee: for whither thou goest, I will go; and whither thou lodgest, I will lodge: thy people shall be my people, and thy God shall be my God: Where thou diest, will I die, an there will I be buried: the Lord do so to me, more also, if ought but death part thee and me." Ruth 1: 1-16(KJV)

"And they told to Mordecai Esther's words. Then Mordecai commanded to answer Esther, think not with thyself that thou shalt escape in the king's house, more than all the Jews. For if thou altogether holdest thy peace at this time, then shall there enlargement and deliverance arise to the Jews from another place; but thou and thy father's house shall be destroyed: and who knoweth whether thou art come to the kingdom for such a time as this?

Then Esther bade them return Mordecai this answer,

"Go, gather together all the Jews that are present in Shushan, and fast ye for me, and neither eat nor drink three days, night or day: I also and my maiden will fast likewise; and so will I go in unto the king, which is not according to the law: and if I perish, I perish. So Mordecai went his way, and did according to all that Esther had commanded him." *Esther 4:12-17 (KJV)*

The Responsibilities of the Church

Proof of ministrative duties in the church

Evangelism:

The church still need Evangelist as in the days of the prophets: Philip was a great Evangelist who ministered to the Eunuch, as also were the Apostles Matthew, Mark and Luke were great evangelist in their points on baptism, and in their travels. Stephen was an excellent Evangelist by example of being widely known as being full of the Holy Ghost and wisdom.

The word gifts

The word gifts are duties given to the church for:

"For the perfecting of the saints, for the work of the ministry, for the edifying of the body of Christ:

Till we all come in the unity of the faith, and of the knowledge of the son of God, unto a perfect man, unto the measure of the stature of fulness of Christ." Ephesians 4:12-13 (KJV)

"To know wisdom, and instruction; to perceive the words of understanding; To receive the instruction of wisdom, justice, and judgment, and equity; To give subtilty to the simple, to the young man knowledge and discretion." Proverbs 1:2-4 (KJV

"All scripture is given by inspiration of God, and is profitable for doctrine, for reproof, For correction, for instruction in righteousness. That the man of God may be perfect, thoroughly furnished unto all good works." 2 Timothy 16-17 (KJV)

But (which becometh women professing godliness) with good works." 1ˢᵗ Timothy 2:1-10 (KJV)

Questions from the Author:

Do you consider yourself the weaker vessel in your relationship, or as a woman?

Reflection:

_____

_____

_____

_____

_____

_____

_____

_____

_____

_____

_____

_____

_____

_____

_____

_____

_____

_____

_____

_____

_____

CHAPTER XIV

The Apostle Warning to the Church

The Fading Leaders

As the apostles were moving off the scene: They left us some warnings of things which was sure to come after their departure, that we may take heed to ourselves, and to be able to recognize the signs.

"Now the Spirit speak expressly, that in the later times some shall depart from the faith, giving heed to seducing, spirits, and doctrine of devils; Speaking lies in hypocrisy; having their conscience seared with a hot iron." 1ˢᵗ Timothy 4:1-2 (KJV)

Paul spoke to the elders at Ephesus saying,

"For I not shunned to declare unto you all the counsel of God. Take heed therefore unto yourselves, and to the flock, over the which the Holy Ghost hath made you overseers, to feed the church of God, which He hath purchased with His own blood. For I know this, that after my departing shall grievous wolves enter in among you, not sparing the flock. Also of your own selves shall men arise, speaking perverse things, to draw away disciples after them." Acts 20:27-30(KJV)

John speaks also concerning warnings to the churches of Asia

"Little children, it is the last time: and as you have heard that antichrist shall come, even now are there many antichrist; whereby we know that it is the last time. They went out from us; for if they had been of us, they would no doubt have continued with us: but they went out, that they might be made manifest that they were not all of us." 1ˢᵗ John 2:18-19 (KJV)

The Apostle Peter said:

"But there were false prophets also among the people, even as there shall be false teachers among you, who privily shall bring damnable heresies, even denying the Lord that bought them, and bring upon themselves swift destruction. And many shall follow their pernicious ways; by reason of whom the way of truth shall be evil spoken of." 2ⁿᵈ Peter 2:1,2 (KJV)

"Knowing this first, that there shall come in the last days scoffers, walking after their own lust," 2ⁿᵈ Peter 3:3 (KJV)

The Apostolic Warnings to the Church continues…

The Apostle John said:

"*They went out from us, but they not of us; for is they had been of us, they would no doubt have continued with us: but they went out, that they might be made manifest that they were not all of us.*" *1st John 2:19(KJV)*

"*Beloved, believe not every spirit, but try the spirit s whether they are of God; because many false prophets are gone out into the world.*" *1st John 4:1 (KJV)*

Jude's warning said:

"*For there are certain men crept in unawares, who were before of old ordained to this condemnation, ungodly men, turning the grace of our God into lasciviousness, and denying the only Lord God, and our Lord Jesus Christ.*

But, beloved, remember ye the words which were spoken before of the apostles of our Lord Jesus Christ; how that they told you there should be mockers in the last time, who should walk after their own ungodly lusts. These be they who separate themselves, sensual, having not the spirit." *Jude 4, 17-19 (KJV)*

Jesus Himself gave us warnings concerning the end times, to be aware.

"*For there shall arise false Christ, and false prophets, and shall great signs and wonders; insomuch that, if it were possible, they shall deceive the very elect. For many shall come in my name, saying, I am Christ, and shall deceive many. And many false Christ shall arise and deceive many,"* Matthew 24:24, 5, 11, (KJV)

The Apostles were aware of the times and the minds that they have had to wrestle with, and how in the later days weak ministers would arise, and deceive many for a lack of knowledge, and that the simple minded would be their first line of prey.

"Paul reminds Timothy and Titus of the one doctrine, and that no other doctrine should ever be preached other than that which he had taught them. He said to Timothy;

If any man teach otherwise, and consent not to wholesome words, even the words of our Lord Jesus Christ, and to the doctrine which as according to godliness, from such withdraw thyself." 1st *Timothy 6:3,5 (KJV)*

The Apostolic Warning

Paul said for us to guard what we have learned:

"Therefore we ought to give the more earnest heed to the things which we have heard, lest at any time we should let them slip. For if the word spoken by angles was steadfast, and every transgression and disobedience received a just reward; How shall we escape, if we neglect so great salvation; which at the first began to be spoken by the Lord, and was confirmed unto us by them that heard Him." Hebrew 2:1-3 (RJV)

Peter's second epistle

"This second epistle, beloved, I now write unto you; in both which I stir up your pure minds by way of remembrance: That ye may be mindful of the words which were spoken before by the holy prophets, and of the commandments of us the apostles of the Lord and saviour:" 2nd Peter 3: 1-2 (KJV)

The Apostle John told us:

"For many deceivers are entered into the world, who confess not that Jesus Christ is come in the flesh. This is deceiver and an anti-Christ. Look to yourselves, that we lose not those things which we both wrought, but that we receive a full reward. Whosoever transgresseth, and abideth not in the doctrine of Christ, hath not God. Ye that abideth in the doctrine of Christ, he hath both the Father and the Son. If there come any unto you, and bring not this doctrine, receive him not into your house, neither bid them God speed, For he that biddeth him God speed is partaker of his evil deeds."
II John 7-11 (KJV)

Isaiah's command

Isaiah tells us: "to seek ye out of the book of the Lord and read." Isaiah 34:16

Paul tells Timothy: *"Till I come, give attendance to reading, to exhortation, to doctrine. Neglect not the gift that is in thee, which was given thee by prophecy, with the laying on of the hands of the presbytery Meditate upon these things;*

give thyself wholly to them; that thy profiting may appear to all. Take heed unto thyself, and unto the doctrine; continue in them: for in doing this thou shalt both save thyself, and them that hear thee." 1ˢᵗ Timothy 4:13 -16 (KJV)

The Apostolic Warnings

Looking at the times and churches

The seven churches addressed in Revelation chapters 2 and 3: they represent the types and conditions of the churches in all generations. From the apostolic warnings we found that many unqualified men and women would, and did come into the ministry.

"For the scriptures saith: "to the law and the testimony: if they speak not according to this word, it is because there is no light in them." Isaiah 8:20 (KJV)

Paul said to Timothy:

"If any man teach otherwise, and consent not to wholesome words, even the words of our Lord Jesus Christ, and to the doctrine which according to godliness; He is proud, knowing nothing, but doting about questions and strifes of words, whereof cometh envy, strife, railings, evil surmisings, Perverse disputing of men of corrupt minds, and destitute of the truth, supposing that gain is godliness: from such withdraw thyself." 1ˢᵗ Timothy 6:3-5) KJV)

These are the men which crept into the churches after the departure of the apostles; Beginning with the last part of the apostolic age. Continuing with the history of the Ephesian church doing their relaxed period; from A.D. 30-100. They being the church that had a zeal for God had left their first love. They had become relaxed, and caught up with other doctrines and other peoples beliefs, and began to practice the doctrine of men. There were some there, which practiced the deeds of the Nicolaitans. The admonishment was that they should repent ot else he would remove their candlestick from among them.

The scriptures said:

"I know thy works, and thy labour, and thy patience, and how thou canst not bear them which are evil: and thou hast tried them which say they are apostles, and are not, and hast found them liars: And hast borne, and hast patience, and for my name's sake hast labored, and hast not fainted. Nevertheless I have somewhat against thee, because thou hast left thy first love. Remember therefore from whence thou art fallen, and repent, and do the first works; or else I will come unto thee quickly and I will remove thy candlestick out of His place, except thou repent. But this thou hast, that thou hatest the deeds of the Nicolaitans, which I hate also. He that hath an ear, let him hear what the spirit saith unto the churches; to him that overcometh will I give to eat of the tree of life, which is in the midst of the paradise of God." Revelation 2:2-7 (KJV)

The Apostolic Warnings

"Therefore we are to give the more earnest heed to the things which we have heard lest at any time we should let them slip. For if the word spoken by angels was stedfast, and every transgression and disobedience received a just recompence of reward; How shall we escape, if we neglect so great salvation; which at the first began to be spoken by the Lord, and was confirmed unto us by them that heard Him." Hebrews 2:1-3 (KJV)

Establishing the New Testament Church

In order to be able to talk about the church, we must first determine which church we are speaking about, because there is a great difference between the wilderness church, and the apostolic church. The wilderness church was a congregation of law keepers, or rather, law breakers in the wilderness under Moses and others. Even Jesus prohibited His disciples from ministering to anyone other than the Jews. It being the Jewish church the only church in existence as a nation. This is why I would caution ministers and pastors to be mindful when speaking to the church as: to who was being spoken too: and in what dispensation, and which gospel was being ministered. The doctrine of the Old Testament Church, which was under the law in the desert and in the wilderness or the doctrine of the modern New Testament Church?

Jesus commanded His disciples to preach to the Jews only.

"These twelve Jesus sent forth, and commanded them, saying, go not into the way of the gentiles, and into any city of the Samaritans, enter ye not: But go rather to the lost sheep of the house of Israel. And as ye go, preach, saying, the kingdom of heaven (the kings domain) is at hand." Matthew 10:5-7 (KJV)

Luke called Moses' church the wilderness church:

*"This is that Moses, which said unto the children of Israel, a prophet shall the Lord your God raise up unto you of your brethren, like unto me; Him shall ye hear. This is He, that was in **the church in the wilderness** with the angel which spake to him in the Mount Sina, and with our fathers: who received the lively oracles to give unto us." Acts 7:37-38 (KJV)*

But thank God that the New Testament church is made up of Holy Ghost filled baptized believers in Christ Jesus. It is a nation made up out of many nations; Jews and gentiles in one body; it is the church of the Holy Spirit in the church, the body of Christ, and the Jews and gentiles in one body, without the law which began on the day of Pentecost about AD 30 or 33.

Note

To the praise of the glory of His grace, wherein He hath made us accepted in the beloved. Ephesian 6:1 (KJV)

"For the body is one, and hath many members, and all the members of that one body, being many, are one body: also is Christ. For by one Spirit are we all baptized into one body, whether we be bond or free; and have been all made to drink into one Spirit. For the body is not one member, but many." 1ˢᵗ *Corinthians 12:12-14 (KJV 129*

Establishing the New Testament Church

In Matthew's gospel is where Jesus made a declaration concerning the building of His church, after Peter's acknowledging of who He was by the Holy Spirit. The question is asked of the individual; whom say ye that I am?

Personal confession

"He saith unto them, but whom say ye that I am? And Simon Peter answered and said, "Thou art the Christ, the son of living God. And Jesus answered and said unto him, blessed art thou, Simon Bar-Jona: for flesh and blood hath not revealed it unto thee, but my Father which is in heaven. And I say also unto thee, that thou art Peter, and upon this rock I will build my church; and the gates of hell shall not prevail against it." Matthew 16: 15-18 (KJV)

Jesus makes a great point here before the building of His church: that is, the Church belongs to Him and never to Man, only the ministry of His church is given to the hand of men. And He is the head of the church, the firstfruits from the dead.

And I say unto thee, that thou art Peter, (a stone) and upon this rock I will build (only Jesus can build the church, and not a man, not even Peter.

We know that it is to the Jews first, so the Jews had the opportunity to accept Him first, but Israel as a nation rejected Christ, so God turned to individuals of all nations, as He did Peter. The scriptures said:

"He came unto His own, and His own received Him not. But as many as received Him, to them gave He power to become the sons of God, even to them that believe on His name: Which was born, not of blood, nor of the will of the flesh, nor of the will of man, but of God. And the word was made flesh, and dwelt among us (and we beheld His glory, the glory as of the only begotten of the Father), full of grace and truth. John bare witness of Him, and cried, saying, this was He of whom I spake, He that cometh after me is preferred before me: for He was before me. And of His fulness have all we received, and grace for grace. For the law was given by Moses, but grace and truth came by Jesus Christ." St. John 1:11-17(KJV)

Establishing the New Testament Church

New Testament church

The New Testament church is a body of people called out or brought out of the world, by the Holy Spirit: as Rebekah was called or brought out of her father's house by Abraham's servant Eleazer, representing the Holy Spirit Genesis 24 (KJV)

The Ephesian church is now under consideration; that is. The church which was taught from the apostolic doctrine, the apostles understood the true doctrine of salvation and the process of it. They knew very well that no matter what came up in the different doctrines that this church would survive, simply because it is the true church which Jesus died for.

What the apostles believed and taught

Their message to the world is to hear what is taught, then believe what was taught by the apostles concerning the death burial and resurrection of Jesus Christ. In this New Testament age the apostles taught that everyone must believe in the death, burial and resurrection of Jesus Christ, this means all denominations of religion, with no exceptions as to whether they are universal or not. Mark 16: 15-17 Acts 8:36-37; 10: 34-43 (KJV)

*"And He said unto them, go ye **into all the world**, and preach the **gospel to every creature**. He that believeth and is baptized shall be saved; **but he that believeth not shall be damned**." Mark 16:15(KJV)*

Repentances: *"In the apostle's teachings, repentances was strongly taught, along with baptism, and receiving of the Holy Ghost.*

And the times of this ignorance God winked at; but now commandeth all men every where to repent." Acts 17:30(KJV)

"Then Peter said unto them, repent and be baptized every one of you in the name of Jesus Christ for the remission of sins, and ye shall receive the gift of the Holy Ghost." Acts 2:38(KJV)

"Repent ye therefore, and be converted, that your sins may be blotted out, when the times of refreshing shall come from the presence of the Lord;" Acts 3:19; (KJV)

Establishing the New Testament Church

Baptism

Their baptism wasn't just to go into the water under the titles, or attributes of God; but they had a **specific method of baptism**. And that method was to baptize in the name of Jesus Christ for the remission of sins. The name of Jesus was part of the method to receive the remission of sins. According to: Acts 2:37, 38; 8:12-17; 10:43-44; 19:1-6 (KJV) the Apostles commanded everyone to be baptized in the name of the Father, and of the son, and of the Holy Ghost. Whose name is Jesus.

The Father

"I am come in my Father's name, and ye receive me not: if another shall come in his own name, him ye will receive." *John 5:43 (KJV)*

The Son

"And she shall bring forth a son, and thou shall call His name Jesus: for He shall save His people from their sins. Behold, a virgin shall be with child, and shall bring forth a son, and they shall call His name Emmanuel, which being interpreted is, God with us." Matthew 1:21, 23 (KJV)

Holy Ghost

*"But the comforter, which is the Holy Ghost, whom the Father will **send in my** (JESUS) **name,** He shall teach you all things, and bring all things to your remembrance, whatsoever I have said unto you." St. John 14:26 (KJV)*

"Jesus tells us that, repentance and remission of sins should be preached in His name, among all nations beginning at Jerusalem." Luke 24:47 (KJV)

*"Be it known unto you all, and to all the people of Israel, that by the name of Jesus Christ of Nazareth, whom ye crucified, whom God raised from the dead, even by Him doth this man stand here before you whole. This is the stone which was set at nought of you builders, which is become the head of the corner. Neither is there salvation in any other: **for there is none other name under heaven given among men, whereby we MUST be saved."** Acts 4:10-12*

Baptism in the Holy Ghost:

The apostles believed and taught that a person should be filled or baptized in the Holy Ghost: after their conversion, after they believed in the death, burial and resurrection of Jesus Christ. The Apostles taught that the Holy Ghost was given after you believed:

Paul asked the disciples at Ephesus that great question.

"He said unto them, have ye received the Holy Ghost **since ye believed?** *Acts 19:1-6 (KJV) (Not when ye believed, but* **since ye believed.) Which saith after the fact).** *And they said unto him, we have not so much as heard whether there be any Holy Ghost."* **Here we see that they have believed, but they have not received the Holy Ghost as yet. The same things happened with the Samaritans in.** *Acts 8:12-15 (KJV)*

Then another question was asked.

"And he said unto them, unto what then were ye baptized? And they said, unto John's baptism.

Now we hear that it is important as to how you are baptized, in other words, baptizing must be with a prescribed formula and mode: to what then were you baptized? And they said unto John's baptism.

Then said Paul, John verily baptized with the baptism of repentance, saying unto the people, that they should believe on Him which should come after him, that is, on Christ Jesus.

It is plain that John's baptism was out of date, and that Jesus baptism was the baptism to be applied to the sinner in washing. Remember, this is called John's baptism. Matthew 3: 11 (KJV) 1ˢᵗ Corinthians 10:2 (KJV) is Moses's baptism.

John said: *I indeed baptize you with water unto repentance: but He that cometh after me is mightier than I, whose shoes I am not worthy to bear: He shall baptize you with the Holy Ghost and with fire:" John 3:11 (KJV)*

So now we must be baptized in Jesus's name putting on Christ: and receiving the gift of the Holy Ghost. This is His promise being fulfilled.

"And when they heard this, they were baptized in the name of Lord Jesus. And when Paul had laid his hands on them, the Holy Ghost came on them; and they spake with tongues, and prophesied." Acts 19: 1-6 (KJV)

It was necessary for the Apostles to hear the utterance as evidence of their infilling: which says, God is come into the body.

"This is a written demonstration of what should happen, after one's conversion and infilling of the Holy Ghost." Acts 19:1-6 (KJV)

Before we can become saved and a part of His body: we must first trust in Him.

"That we should be to the praise of His glory, who first trusted in Christ. In whom ye also trusted, after that ye heard the word of truth, the gospel of your salvation: in whom also after that ye believed, ye were seal with that holy spirit of promise, Which is the earnest of our inheritance until the redemption of the purchased possession, unto the praise of His glory." Ephesian 1: 12-14 (KJV)

The Godhead: The apostles also believed in only one God:

"But to us there is but one God, the Father, of whom are all things, and we in Him; and one Lord Jesus Christ, by whom are all things and we by Him." 1ˢᵗ Corinthians 8:6 (KJV)

And that He was manifested in the body of Jesus Christ.

"And that Christ is that one God." John 1:1, 2, 10, 14 (KJV)

For in Him dwelleth all the fulness of the Godhead bodily. Colossian 2:9; (KJV)

"And without controversy great is the mystery of godliness: God was manifest in the flesh, Justified in the spirit, seen of

angels, preached unto the gentiles, believed on in the world, received up into glory." 1ˢᵗ. Timothy 3:16 (KJV)

Holiness: the Apostles believed in holy living to those who were saved, and washed in the blood of Jesus

"But as He which hath called you is holy, so be ye holy in all manner of conversation; Because it is written, be ye holy; for I am holy. 1ˢᵗ. Peter 1: 15- 16; James 5:15-16(KJV)

The Apostles taught what they received from Jesus; which saith:

"This second epistle, beloved, I now write unto you; in both in which I stir up your pure minds by way of remembrance: That you may be mindful of the words which was spoken before by the holy prophets, and of the commandments of us the apostles of the Lord and saviour: Knowing this first, that there shall come in the last days scoffers, walking after their own lusts." 2ⁿᵈ Peter 3: 1-3 (KJV)

We are commanded to contend for the faith

*"Beloved, when I gave all diligence to write unto you of the common salvation, it was needful for me to write unto you, and exhort you that **you should earnestly contend for the faith which was ONCE** delivered unto the saints." Jude 3(KJV)*

"As I besought thee to abide at Ephesus, when I went into Macedonia, that thou mightiest charge some that they teach no other doctrine." 1ˢᵗ. Timothy 1:3(KJV)

"And the things that thou hast heard of me among many witnesses, the same commit thou to faithful men, who shall be able to teach others also." 2nd Timothy 2:2(KJV)

"For I testify unto every man that heareth the words of the prophecy of this book, if any man shall add unto these things, God shall add unto him the plagues that are written in this book." Revelation 22:18 (KJV)

Doctrine: a subject or lesson that is taught, the basic of a foundation, salvation: a way to escape, evil or people, bringing one into a safe heaven.

Refreshing the mind

I have concluded that the doctrine of salvation covers the entire bible and all the people: from Genesis 3:15 forward; where God promised man redemption, and promised Satan his destruction, after the disobedience of Adam. Since that time to this present moment the war still rages over the man's soul, per se. The son of God Luke 3:38 (KJV) even moreso over the church as the bride: God's church: His glory

This is not soul salvation, but body salvation

Noah and Moses gave us an example of salvation through the head of the house or the family.

Moses as a type of Christ, brought salvation to his people through the Red Sea crossing. Noah brought salvation to his house, as did Moses by the word of the Lord, Noah through the Ark as the church. But the gospel of Jesus Christ brought soul saving salvation in His dispensation to all people through His blood sacrifice at Calvary. This was His grand display of the infinite love of God.

"For God so loved the world that He gave His only begotten son…" *John 3:16 (KJV)*

In all of its encouragement; having nothing but mercy; it is not exclusive to the Jew nor to the gentile only, but it embraces the whole human race. Jesus, the sinner's friend: for He is the mediator of the New Covenant, which is ratified by His blood. We are saved by grace, through faith in His blood.

"Therefore as by the offence of one man judgment came upon all men to condemnation; even so by the righteousness of one the free gift came upon all men unto justification of life. For as by one man's disobedience many were made sinners, so by the obedience of one shall many be made righteous." *Romans 5:18, 19) (KJV)*

Step one in the dispensation of Jesus Christ begins with Jesus coming to save His people, and the world from their sins, Matthew 1:21 (KJV) and He asked the question of His disciples; whom do men say that I am, Matthew 16:13 (KJV) Then the second personal question is, **whom do you say** that I am? Matthew 16:15 (KJV) This is where it was revealed to Peter and to the world through revelation of the Holy Ghost: that this was Jesus called Christ, meaning the Messiah. God come in the flesh according to St. John 1:1; 14; 10 (KJV) to redeem all of humanity from the hand of Satan.

Our salvation must need come through the faith that we have in His sacrifice at Calvary, in the death burial and resurrection of Jesus Christ. We had to hear of His sacrifice at Calvary, after we heard, we had to believe this with our whole heart, and that it is most suited, to all the wants and wishes of every soul of man. We are to take heed not to refuse Jesus as our Lord and saviour, in His calling us to salvation by His gospel out of His love for mankind; He gave His life for all, and is still our intercessor between God and man as our mediator.

Hear well these words

"See that ye refuse not Him that speaketh. For if they escaped not who refused Him that spake on earth, much more shall not we escape, if we turn away from Him that speaketh from Heaven:" Hebrews 12:25 (KJV)

"According as He hath chosen us in Him before the foundation of the world, that we should be holy and without blame before Him in love: Having predestined us unto the adoption of children by Jesus Christ to Himself, according to the good pleasure of His will. To the praise of the glory of His grace, wherein He hath made us accepted in the beloved. In whom we have redemption through His blood, the forgiveness

of sin, according to the riches of His grace." Ephesians 1:4-7 (KJV)

All the scriptures bring us to repentance, that we might be saved: Paul and Peter both said that we had to repent of our sins, which meant that one of the steps to salvation was to repent. Romans 10:9; Acts 2:38(KJV)

Romans said: "that if thou shalt confess with thy mouth the Lord Jesus, and shall believe in thine heart that God hath raised Him from the dead, thou shalt be saved. Then Peter said unto them, repent, and be baptized every one of you in the name of Jesus Christ for the remission of sins, and ye shall receive the gift of the Holy Ghost." Romans 10:9; Acts 2:38 (KJV)

The next step to our salvation was to be baptized, and to be filled with the Holy Ghost, and to live a Christian life. This is the foundation for salvation, coming from Jesus through the apostle's doctrine, as we saw from the beginning, the man's place is in the leadership of the household's salvation.

"Much more then, being now justified by His blood, we shall be saved from wrath through Him. For if, when we were enemies, we were reconciled to God by the death of His Son, much more, being reconciled, we shall be saved by His life. And not only so, but we also joy in God through our Lord Jesus Christ, by whom we have now received the atonement." Romans 5:9-11(KJV)

My Conclusion on Refreshing the Mind

"And all things are of God, who hath reconciled us to Himself by Jesus Christ, and hath given us the ministry of reconciliation:

To wit, that God was in Christ, reconciling the world unto Himself, not imputing their trespasses unto them; and hath committed unto us the word of reconciliation.

Now then we are ambassadors for Christ, as though God did beseech you by us: we pray you in Christ stead, be ye reconciled to God.

For He hath made Him to be sin for us, who knew no sin; that we might be made the righteousness of God in Him." *2nd Corinthians 5:18-21 (KJV)*

I conclude that it is still the man's responsibility to lead and support the family, as it was previously **appointed unto him**. To lead and guide the household in knowledge and in righteousness unto salvation as Christ leads His Church, being the responsible husband and father which constitutes the family, and the wife will be happy to follow the man and be content to live with him in all faithfulness.

This concludes my documentary.

Can't be Reasoned

"As I besought thee to abide still at Ephesus, when I went to Macedonia, that thou mightiest charge some that they teach no other doctrine," 1ˢᵗ. *Timothy 1: 3(KJV)*

Because salvation is something that a man can't reason out in his mind, or put his hand too, it is sometimes unacceptable to him. But this is why it is God's salvation alone with no input from man. If man had any part to add to this process, then it would be variations to this process according to how man wants to live, and there is none, only God's.

Clarification of the word

No traces

In reference to the remission of sins; the baptism in the name of Jesus Christ is the applying of His blood to our sins, removing all previous stain of sin, leaving no traces with God. There is no record to be brought up before you again, ever. Thy record is clear.

"Come now, and let us reason together, saith the LORD: though your sins be as scarlet, they shall be as white as snow; though they be red like crimson, they shall be as wool." Isaiah *1: 18(KJV)*

"For I will be merciful to their unrighteousness, and their sins and their iniquities will I remember no more." Hebrews 8:12(KJV)

"Whom God hath set forth to be a propitiation through faith in His blood, to declare His righteousness for the remission of sins that are past, through the forbearance of God;" Romans 3:25 (KJV)

This is the complete process of salvation when we have not only passed through the steps of salvation, but it is when we have been totally redeemed, recovered, and clear of sin and transgressions. Paul said:

"For behold this selfsame thing, ye sorrowed after a godly sort, what carefulness it wrought in you, yea, what clearing of yourselves, yea, what indignation, yea, what fear, yea, what vehement desire, yea, what zeal, yea, what revenge! In all things ye have approved yourselves to be clear in this matter." 2nd Corinthians 7:11 (KJV)

Questions from the Author:

Are you living a sinners lifestyle as a Christian. If so, what message does that send to others, and how does that bless you or your God? As women, let us re-fine ourselves and pray everyday for all people, and especially for our men; they need us to stand before God on their behalf in our weakness for them. Always show love, we as the weaker vessel keeps growing stronger in Jesus.

Reflection:

_____

_____

_____

_____

_____

_____

_____

_____

_____

_____

_____

_____

_____

_____

_____

_____

_____

_____

DEDICATION

This book is dedicated to all the females of this world; young and old alike. **Know this,** we are God's chosen representatives as His Church. The woman (as the Church) has been attacked from all sides.

She has been assaulted by Satan, men of this world, each other, and false doctrine. Yet, in all of this she has been saved by God; by His grace through faith in His blood through Jesus Christ, and His redemptive process. His Church is continually birthing more and more souls into His body daily.

The female being wounded: and considered the weaker vessel, has not been weakened in her foundation as the Church, be encouraged we are still His chosen vessel for greatness as His Church.

Printed in the United States
By Bookmasters